Healing the Angry Heart

A Strategy for Confident Mothering

by Kathy Collard Miller

Aglow Publications
A Ministry of Women's Aglow Fellowship, Int'l.
P.O. Box 1548
Lynnwood, WA 98046-1558
USA

To my parents,
Richard and Vivian,
for their love and support.

Cover design by David Marty

Unless otherwise indicated, Scripture quotations are from the New American Standard Bible, © The Lockman Foundation 1960, 1962, 1963, 1968, 1971, 1972, 1973, 1975, and are used by permission. Other Scripture quotations are from The Living Bible (TLB), © 1971 by Tyndale House Publishers, Wheaton, Illinois, and are used by permission; the Good News Bible (GNB); the King James Version (KJV); and the Revised Version (RSV).

ISBN 0-932305-68-7

Table of Contents

SECTION IV
Discipline Your Child Effectively

SECTION V
Rebuild Yourself and Your Child

Introduction

"I don't know why I get so angry all the time. I have lots to be thankful for. I have healthy kids and a good husband. But I get so upset with my youngest boy, who is seven. I have to get after him so often. He doesn't tie his shoes or listen to me half the time. He is the child who acts most like me.

"I know I expect too much from my kids. I know I make a lot of mistakes, but I don't want my kids to. I have to tell them to do something three or four times. Then I threaten them, but they don't care. I get so mad because I have to talk to them over and over again.

"I hate the way I am, but I don't know what to do about it. I look real sweet on the outside, but I'm full of hate and jealousy inside. When I was little, my mother always gave me anything I wanted; even so, I was mean to her. My kids are treating me the same way, but I don't want them to turn out like me.

"The root of my problem is me. I've never learned to give of myself, yet people use me. I can't say no but after I say yes I hate myself for it.

"I don't like myself, so I take it out on my kids. I don't hit them much, but I'm always putting them down and screaming at them.

"I want to learn how to control my anger. I want to learn how I can help my kids listen and do what I ask. I'm willing to try anything to change."

When I received this letter from Julie, I wept. I wanted to fly immediately to her city, wrap my arms around her and infuse into her the hope and confidence that she can change, with help. But I couldn't do that. I could only write to her, encourage her to get professional counseling and tell her I would be praying for her.

As I meditated on her letter, longing to help her, I realized

7

that she represents the hurt, anguish and guilt of countless other angry parents. Then I cried again.

I acutely identify with women who struggle with their anger, because at one time I was overwhelmed with guilt about the way I treated my daughter when she was two years old. At times, when rage blinded my self-control and reason, I choked, slapped, kicked and hit her. I hated myself for what I was doing and cried out to God. He didn't give me instantaneous victory, but over a period of about a year, He helped me see the causes of my anger and apply the solutions that worked for me.

So I understand how parents can be overwhelmed by anger and frustration. I know how a mother feels when she's all dressed up to go out and the baby spits up on her dress. Or when one child is having a temper tantrum and clinging to her leg while she is trying to change a nine-month-old's diaper . . . and the phone rings. She wants to rip her leg away from her toddler, run out the door screaming, enter the solace of her car and drive about 1,000 miles away.

How can a mother cope with her frustrations? She probably does not feel free to share them at her Bible study on Monday morning. Instead, she, and everyone else, arrives looking her best, every hair in place, Bible study done and smile plastered on. Will anyone admit that she had to get up at four A.M. that morning to do her Bible study, because she didn't have time the week before? Will another mother confess that she spanked her child in anger that morning because she was hassled trying to get two kids and herself ready? Will anyone break her frozen smile to tell the group that she fears her husband may be having an affair with his young secretary?

Probably not. Unfortunately, it is hard to find Bible study groups, Sunday school classes or church groups in which feelings, fears, anger and disappointments are shared. But without that openness, the mother who feels down that day cannot receive comfort, encouragement and instruction.

More often, the young mother walks around thinking she is the only one who gets angry with her child, the only one who doesn't trust the Lord all the time, the only one who is so utterly exhausted that her greatest wish is to sleep for a whole day without hearing the familiar, "Mommy, MOMMY!" She is fed up with trying to be Super Person, Super Mom and Super Christian.

If you have experienced similar feelings, this book will help you see that you are not alone. It also offers practical ideas on how to cope with the anger, frustration, loneliness and ambivalent feelings that occur when love becomes anger. We will see that how we view ourselves affects how we react to anger temptations. We will look at anger itself and examine why we react with irritation instead of understanding and patience. We also will examine stressful circumstances and discover ways to handle life when everything seems to be falling apart around us. In addition, we'll learn different ways to discipline our children so that we'll be in control of ourselves. And we will discuss ways to rebuild ourselves, our children and our relationships with them.

I'm confident that as you read this book, you'll rejoice as did my friend Betty, who recently wrote, "It's so wonderful to know I'm not the only mother who experiences unpleasant feelings." And as you apply these ideas, you'll find that anger and frustration need not control your life.

Section I

Put Esteem Back Into Self-Image

Chapter 1

Anger Begins With Low Self-Esteem

Laurie grew up in her grandmother's home, because her mother didn't want to raise her. Whenever she was with her mother, her mother told her what a bad girl she was and that she wouldn't amount to anything.

As a teenager, Laurie lacked confidence and constantly thought, *You're no good. You'll never do anything good with your life. You're a failure no matter what you try.* When she met Phillip and he said he loved her, she believed he was the answer to her self-hatred, and she married him. But even his love didn't blot out her belittling memories.

When her first child, a daughter, was born prematurely with multiple physical problems, many people prayed for her and she survived. Now Laurie could love another human being and see her love returned by this baby who needed her so much. Three years later, the birth of their son completed their family.

But soon the burden and stress of caring for two children overwhelmed Laurie. The lack of love during her own childhood hindered her ability to provide for her children's emotional needs. The children's temper tantrums communicated to Laurie that she wasn't a good mother. Her feelings of inadequacy and frustration caused her to lash out at them with physical and verbal rages.

Realizing that she needed help, Laurie gathered together all her courage to admit her problem and seek professional counseling. Today she is working through her childhood rejection, but she hasn't found instant deliverance.

"At times, I use all my emotional strength to cope with the demands of a family and a home, and then I can't cope any more," she says. "I yell at the children and spank them until bruises form on their bottoms. I don't think I give them any emotional nourishment at all. Sometimes I wake up in the morning with so much anger, but I don't even know where it comes from. I stay angry throughout the day and I don't know why. I know the Lord is frowning on my situation. Since our daughter survived, I figured God must have something really special in mind for her, but I'm ruining that special plan. I love the Lord, but it's hard for me to believe He loves me when I behave wrong."

Laurie, at thirty years of age, is experiencing the repercussions of the poor self-image she developed as a child. This burdens her emotional strength and reduces her ability to cope with even the slightest stress. Most likely, it will take many hours of counseling and months, maybe years, of painful daily decisions to overcome the handicap of low self-esteem.

Anger Begins With Low Self-Esteem

HOW DOES SELF-IMAGE AFFECT ANGER?

We are talking about self-esteem before we directly address anger, because self-image and self-esteem are the most powerful forces affecting how we deal with anger. When we don't feel good about ourselves, when our self-esteem is low, then we are more prone to act in anger. When we perceive ourselves accurately, when our self-image is correct and we recognize that we are valuable and worthy of love, then we can cope with the inevitable temptations to react in anger. So let's first define self-image and self-esteem.

Self-image is how I see myself and it encompasses the view that I think others have of me. I may see myself as patient or prone to anger, compassionate or intolerant, loving or critical, ambitious or lazy, self-controlled or impulsive, friendly or shy, and as possessing many other characteristics. My image includes how I view myself physically, as attractive or homely, too tall or too short, petite or husky, etc.

Most of these evaluations are subtle and may never even enter my consciousness. Even so, they still affect how I see myself, and as a result, how I respond and react to people and circumstances.

Self-esteem is slightly different; it is my evaluation of myself and my degree of belief, respect and confidence in myself. Do I believe I'm worthy of love from God and others? Do I have confidence that what I attempt I will succeed? Do I like who I am and what I am becoming? All these ideas are part of what we think of ourselves. In Romans 12:3, Paul cautioned each of his readers "not to think more highly of himself than he ought to think; but to think so as to have sound judgment, as God has allotted to each a measure of faith."

Having a good self-image and high self-esteem means having good judgment about who I am. It's a matter of accurately

15

and honestly assessing my strengths and weaknesses and then giving God the credit for how He is using those strengths and correcting those weaknesses.

A poor self-image can result from being taught to be "lowly and humble" because we are "nothing." Pride, on the other hand, claims that the good things we do result from our own effort and strength, rather than from God working through us. When someone like Laurie thinks, *I'm no good,* she has low self-image and false humility. If she thought instead, *I made a mistake, but I'm going to learn from it and depend on the Lord next time so I won't make the same mistake,* she would be thinking with sound judgment. That would indicate she had a healthy self-image, not easily destroyed by failure and not puffed up by success.

Unfortunately, I did not have that kind of self-image when my daughter, Darcy, was two years old and Mark was newborn. As a result, my emotional strength was very limited. When it was overtaxed by the demands of motherhood, I reacted in anger and rage. In my book, *Out of Control,* I tell how God helped me overcome my abusive anger toward my daughter.

During that process I realized that self-image is not something we can build by ourselves. It comes from accepting love from others. Even if we think no one else loves us (which may or may not be true), we can look to our Heavenly Father. When we *fully realize* and *fully accept* how much God loves us, then our self-esteem can become healthy and growing. *The key is for us simply to accept His love, because He loves us unconditionally no strings attached.*

God may not work in your life as He did in mine. In fact, I can almost guarantee He won't (at least, not exactly). I don't know what method He will use to build your self-esteem, but

I do know, without a doubt, that He wants to build it.

Because God is creative, He uses many different ways to build us up. Dianne experienced His handiwork after she became too severe in spanking her two daughters.

Dianne had carried a belittling self-image into adulthood. Even though her parents would say that no one's daughter was more loved than Dianne, she somehow hadn't received their love. After she married and her two daughters were born, she became suicidal. Then she looked for a Christian counselor to help her.

She explains, "I can't think of specific ways God improved my self-image, but I know it was strengthened, as other things became better. You see, low self-esteem affects all other areas, like relationships with a spouse, friends, kids . . . whatever. As I learned to love myself, I could love others. I also realized that God wasn't too busy for me, and He loved me and accepted me where I was at. But this realization was a process that took time.

"One reason I wanted to kill myself was knowing I would go to be with the Lord and be loved by Him in heaven. I didn't want to hurt anyone, even myself; I just longed to be loved by Jesus even if it meant suicide. When my counselor helped me recognize that people on earth loved me and could satisfy that deep desire to be loved, then suicide wasn't so appealing. Finally I accepted that my husband could meet that need if I would let him."

Dianne discovered an important concept: Each of us needs to accept love from others if we are to feel loved and to build our self-esteem. It's a choice, and often a difficult one.

The problem is, we often don't recognize when someone else offers us love because they aren't loving us the way we want to be loved or through something that we identify as love.

17

Healing the Angry Heart

For instance, perhaps a woman enjoys receiving flowers from her husband and thinks of that as love. But her husband thinks giving flowers is a waste of money. He believes he is showing his love by working overtime and providing extras for his family. In contrast, she interprets his willingness to work overtime as meaning he doesn't want to spend time with her, so she complains about his being gone so much.

The wife may not share her love as her husband wants her to, either. She may bake him pies or fix gourmet meals, taking it for granted that he sees her love in all her busyness. The husband, on the other hand, loves simple food and thinks, "If she would get out of the kitchen and make love to me, I'd know for sure that she loves me."

These misinterpretations can start a cycle of bitterness, unhappiness and unfulfilled needs.

The same thing can happen with our children. When my daughter, Darcy, was eight years old, she started an annoying habit of jumping up and gently hitting the top of my head. Every time she did this (with the silliest grin on her face), I became irritated and told her to stop, but she continued to do it.

Then I realized she was doing this to show her love. It was her way of paying attention to me and, of course, of getting my attention. She felt uncomfortable showing love by doing what I thought was acceptable, such as hugging and kissing me, so she tapped my head instead. As soon as I viewed this as her demonstration of love, it didn't irritate me any more, and I would reach out and hug her. Recently she stopped doing it, and I've noticed that she has been more willing to hug instead.

Is it possible that your husband, children, parents or friends are trying to express their love to you, but you don't view it as love? Maybe your mother calls more often than you'd like.

18

You look at it as meddling; she thinks she's showing love and concern. Maybe your child keeps making a bouquet for you out of a neighbor's beautiful flower garden; all you see is the disobedience and your neighbor's anger. (This doesn't mean your child shouldn't be told not to pick a neighbor's flowers, but perhaps you could direct him to your garden.)

A good discussion starter for a husband and wife, or even friends, is "I would like you to show me your love by . . ." or, "I'm showing you my love when I. . . ." With greater communication, we each can receive the love more often that others are offering and, in turn, we can show others the kind of love that they desire.

GOD'S LOVE

We also often misinterpret God's love. When we look at how He made us and we see our physical imperfections or personality weaknesses, or we remember the pain of an unhappy childhood, we might think that God doesn't love us very much; otherwise He would not have saddled us with such burdens. But the truth is, "God doesn't make junk!"

When I first heard that saying, I found it hard to believe because of all the faults, insecurities and sins that oppressed me. Eventually, as I began to comprehend the truth of that statement, I could love and accept myself. I really began to believe that since God made me, I wasn't junky!

God made you, too, and He wants your estimation of yourself to be as He regards you: important, valuable and loved.

Psalm 139:13-18 (LB) says:

"You made all the delicate, inner parts of my body, and knit them together in my mother's womb. Thank You for making me so wonderfully complex! It is amazing to think about. Your workmanship is marvelous—and how well I know it.

19

Healing the Angry Heart

You were there while I was being formed in utter seclusion! You saw me before I was born and scheduled each day of my life before I began to breathe. Every day was recorded in Your Book!

"How precious it is, God, to realize that You are thinking about me constantly! I can't even count how many times a day Your thoughts turn towards me. And when I waken in the morning, You are still thinking of me!"

God created you for His purpose and plan. No matter what your past represents, you can accept and love yourself, because God does! If you reject yourself, you are saying, "God made junk!" Isaiah 45:9 encourages us to submit to the workmanship of our Heavenly Father: "Woe to the man who fights with his Creator. Does the pot argue with its maker? Does the clay dispute with him who forms it, saying, 'Stop, you're doing it wrong!' or the pot exclaim, 'How clumsy can you be!'?"

Once we accept how God made us, we can concentrate on how He shows us His love. His primary way was by sending His son, Jesus, to die for our sins. When we acknowledge that we have sinned and trust in Jesus to take the punishment we deserve, God forgives us and adopts us as His children. Then we are entitled to wonderful rights and privileges that make us important and special.

Our first privilege is that we can come to God at any time to talk with Him or request something, knowing He always will answer, "Yes," "No," or "Wait." We also have God's promise that He will not allow anything to come into our lives except that which we can handle in Jesus' power and which He can use for our good (see 1 Corinthians 10:13 and Romans 8:28).

In addition, God gives us His Holy Spirit to empower us to

live a life of obedience to Him. His Spirit also produces in us wonderful character traits, such as "love, joy, peace, patience, kindness, goodness, faithfulness, gentleness, self-control" (Galatians 5:22,23). With these qualities, we can experience the abundant life Jesus promises in John 10:10b.

Furthermore, we can experience God's forgiveness and cleansing any time we sin simply by confessing it (1 John 1:9). And we can trust God for every aspect of our lives (Proverbs 3:5,6).

As I meditate on these privileges that make you and me special, I realize our great worth, which is so much more than we ever could imagine, just like the violin in Myra Brooks Welch's poem, "Touch of the Master's Hand":

'Twas battered and scarred, and the auctioneer
Thought is scarcely worth his while,
To waste much time on the old violin
But he held it up with a smile.
What am I bid for the old violin?
Who'll start the bidding for me?
A dollar—two dollars! And who'll make it three?
Three dollars once, three dollars twice,
Going for three, but no:
From the room far back a gray-haired man
Came forward and picked up the bow
And wiping the dust from the old violin
And tightening the loosened strings,
He played a melody, pure and sweet,
Like a caroling angel sings.

Healing the Angry Heart

Then the music stopped, and the auctioneer,
In a voice now subdued and low,
Said, "What am I bid for the old violin,"
And he held it up with the bow.
"A thousand dollars!" And who'll make it two?
"Two thousand?" And who'll make it three?
"Three thousand once; three thousand twice,
Going, and gone," cried he.
And the people cheered, but some of them cried.
"We do not understand;
What changed its worth?"
Quick came the reply, "The touch of the master's hand."

And there's many a man with life out of tune;
Battered and scarred by sin,
That's auctioned cheap to a thoughtless crowd,
Much like the old violin.
A mess of pottage, a glass of wine,
A game, and he travels on.
He's going once, he's going twice,
He's going and almost gone.
But the Master comes, and the foolish crowd
Can never quite understand, the worth of a soul
And the change that's wrought
By the touch of the Master's hand.

WHAT YOU CAN DO

1. Make a sign that says, "God Doesn't Make Junk!" and post it on your bathroom mirror.
2. Memorize Psalm 139:14: "I will give thanks to Thee, for I am fearfully and wonderfully made; wonderful are Thy works, and my soul knows it very well."

Chapter 2

A Distortion of Christian Perfection

Perfectionism and negative self-talk are two of the most common ways we distort our view of ourselves (our self-image). In this chapter, we'll talk about perfectionism; in the next, we'll deal with self-talk.

Psychotherapist Karen Horney calls perfectionism "the tyranny of the ought." Sharon, mother of a fifteen-month-old, lives under that emotional dictator. She is controlled by lists, achievements and a spotless home. A beautiful woman with faultless makeup and coordinated wardrobe, she wants to be the very best person she can be for her own sake and for her Lord Jesus.

She writes down what she wants to accomplish in a day, but sees the afternoon slip by before she has crossed off all the projects. Frustration begins to build, tension causes her neck muscles to tighten, and when her toddler spills her milk or disobeys, Sharon flames into curses at her and wishes she could return to her childless days.

This Christian woman experiences a constant dissatisfaction with what she does and who she is. Always striving to be better, she picks out and concentrates on her slightest error, even when her behavior was acceptable. Her three most frequent thoughts about herself are, *I could have done better; I should have reacted this way;* and *I would have acted differently if only....*

Besides feeling dissatisfied with herself, she also has the vague feeling that God is never quite persuaded that she is doing all she can to live for Him. When she remembers how Jesus died for her sins, she condemns herself even more. After all that He has done for her, she should pray more, be a better witness and apply biblical instruction with greater wisdom.

It wasn't until Sharon began to understand the difference between perfectionism and Christian perfection that she could accept herself as a person and as a child of God. Perfectionism is that sense of needing to perform to earn God's acceptance. In contrast, Christian perfection is knowing we are accepted because of the forgiveness we receive when we ask Jesus to be our Lord and Savior.

David Seamands in his book, *Healing for Damaged Emotions,* says, "There is a great difference between true Christian perfection and perfectionism. Perfectionism is a counterfeit for Christian perfection, holiness, sanctification, or the Spirit-filled life. Instead of making us holy persons and integrated personalities—that is, whole persons in Christ—perfectionism leaves us spiritual Pharisees and emotional neurotics. There is only one ultimate cure for perfectionism: It is as profound and yet as simple as the word grace."[1]

A Distortion of Christian Perfection

As Christians, God totally accepts us, so we no longer need to try to earn salvation or acceptance. In His eyes, we are perfect because we are covered with a mantle of grace.

But we do not live perfectly, because we are still human, and our old nature wars against the Holy Spirit within us. Nevertheless, we need not be discouraged; God is more interested in our progress than in our perfection. He simply wants us to keep growing closer to Him.

Even the apostle Paul said late in his life, "Not that I have already obtained it, or have already become perfect, but I press on in order that I may lay hold of that for which also I was laid hold of by Christ Jesus . . . but one thing I do: forgetting what lies behind and reaching forward to what lies ahead, I press on toward the goal for the prize of the upward call of God in Christ Jesus" (Philippians 3:12-14).

The word *perfect* also can be translated *mature* or *complete*. If anyone could reach perfection or full maturity, we would think that Paul could, yet he said he did not.

Paul goes on to say in verse 15, "Let us therefore, as many as are perfect, have this attitude." In verse 12, he says he's not perfect, then he explains in verse 15 that an attitude of perfection is forgetting what lies behind and pressing on toward the call of God. Therefore, Christian perfection is forgiving and forgetting our mistakes and focusing on becoming more like Jesus by relaxing in the Holy Spirit's power to control us.

Perfectionism is the opposite. Perfectionism concentrates on the past and on striving to do what is right through our own efforts. It results in discouragement and self-condemnation, because we never can measure up in our own power.

Perfectionism can have several causes. Possibly the parents offered only conditional love to their daughter. Even

25

though she has grown up and married, she may not receive acceptance unless she "performs" according to her parents' expectations for perfection.

Perfectionism also can result from a temperament. Melancholy persons tend to be very hard on themselves when they don't perform at their own high standards.

My own struggle against perfectionism stems from my melancholy temperament. My parents were loving, supportive and accepting, yet somehow I never measured up to who I thought I should be and what I thought I should do. I didn't recognize my perfectionism until several years ago when I tried to raise my strong-willed daughter. She helped me see my attitudes for what they really were: unrealistic and perfectionistic.

Therein lies one of perfectionism's problems: We don't always recognize it at first. After all, I did not have unrealistic standards for everything I did, so I didn't classify myself as a perfectionist. I was content to sew an imperfect dress, I could handle preparing a meal that wasn't gourmet, I often allowed a room to stay messy, and if I was hurried enough, I could go out of the house without putting on makeup.

But the standards that were most important to me, such as what other people thought of me, I could not lower. When my daughter didn't behave angelically in public, I became furious later on. If anyone saw that messy room or noticed the flaw in my dress, I felt unacceptable. It was all right for *me* to know of my imperfections, but not for anyone else to, because at the foundation of wanting to be perfect was my knowledge of how inadequate I really was. I constantly tried to say to myself and especially to others, "Look! I am worth something. See how perfectly I do everything?" But inside I still felt inadequate, because I saw myself fail in so many areas. So I tried all the more to be perfect.

My high expectations and feelings of inadequacy boiled to the surface when Darcy demanded more love from me than I thought I possessed. How much love could I give her when I didn't even love myself? It was frustrating. Then, in my efforts to preserve whatever bit of self-esteem I had, I pushed her away. I didn't want her to expose my inadequacy.

This is how perfectionism is connected to self-image. It is merely compensation for inadequacy and a cover-up for poor self-esteem. Through this compensation we strive to become what is impossible without the Holy Spirit's power.

STRIVING VS. RELAXING

We can tell that we are striving in our own power when we are tense, angry, or condemning ourselves. It's like an emotional "gritting of teeth." Now when I begin to feel that kind of tension and effort, I stop, close my eyes, take several deep breaths and imagine the Holy Spirit flowing into me. I focus on who I am in Christ and the power I have as a Christian. As a result, I usually feel a release of that tension and I experience an inner power to react and behave the way the Lord wants me to. I have renewed peace and confidence that God will work in me.

As I rely on God, I sometimes need to give up some expectations that I'd determined were so important, or forgive someone, or remind myself that if I'm late, the world won't cave in. I also may need to review the admonishment to "Cease striving and know that I am God" (Psalm 46:10).

God doesn't want us to try harder; He wants us to relax and believe that He will perform through us. We still have to make choices, but when we focus on the Lord and give Him permission to take over our reactions and desires, He enables us to choose righteously.

27

Healing the Angry Heart

You can tell whether you are striving or relaxing by noticing your emotional reactions. If you are striving, you will experience tension, anger, irritation or other unpleasant feelings. But if you are relaxing in God's control, you'll sense peace, love, self-control and the other fruit of the Spirit (see Galatians 5:22,23).

When I sing in a choir, I'm very aware of the value of relaxing. I'm not a very good vocalist, but when I sing alongside a strong alto, my voice becomes strong and stays on key. I feel relaxed, knowing I have her support.

That's how it is when we cooperate with the Spirit. We relax in His control by believing that He's going to work in and through us.

Paul demonstrated that belief when he wrote, "For I am confident of this very thing, that He who began a good work in you will perfect it until the day of Christ Jesus" (Philippians 1:6).

God has that same confidence for He is the one maturing us. He knows we're in a process of growth and He isn't finished with us yet. But He's not in a hurry, either, because He already views us as finished products, and He knows we'll get there.

Mary is beginning to feel assured that God is changing her. She writes: "I always thought the Lord was providing all my strength, but it's amazing to discover what areas of our lives we hold onto and operate by our own power, rather than by God's. I was touched by that because I realized that I didn't concede to God every part of my life, because of either ignorance or the idea that 'I can handle this area myself; it's too silly an area to bother God with.'

"So I prayed that God would help me recognize my need for His guidance in *all* things. I believe that's what He was (and is) doing. It *has* been hard, but *now* the fruit is beginning to show, and I'm starting to enjoy the kids more and look forward to my time with them. I still have my moments . . . but God is helping me put out the fires and anger much more quickly."

WHAT YOU CAN DO

1. Notice the times that you use the words "should have," "could have" and "would have." Turn your mind around to think, "I'm not perfect and I never will be. God is interested in my progress, so I'm going to learn from my mistake."
2. Memorize Romans 8:1: "There is therefore now no condemnation for those who are in Christ Jesus."

Chapter 3
Changing Negative Self-Talk

Imagine a horror movie about a mad scientist who replaces a person's brain with a tape recording that tells him how to think, react and believe. The scientist can program this human to behave exactly the way he wants him to. His creature goes around doing good, to the delight of others, or behaving wickedly, to the terror of the community, depending upon what the tape squeaks out as it churns in his skull.

Actually, that movie concept already is being performed, but not by Frankenstein—by you and me. Each of us is like a mad scientist, programming our own minds. Without knowing it, we have been recording in our brains all of our lives, and we replay our tapes constantly. As we listen, we form our self-image. As a result, we think, react and believe according to how we talk to ourselves.

31

Healing the Angry Heart

Have you ever responded to someone in a way that you really didn't intend to and walked away thinking, *Why did I act that way?* or *Why did I say that? That's not what I really meant...?*

Those responses result from self-talk. You hadn't been thinking that at the time of the incident, but you had thought it in the past, and you unconsciously had programmed yourself to react that way.

In this chapter we want to look at how that tape recording of our past affects the image we have of ourselves, and how we can change it.

CORRECTING NEGATIVE SELF-TALK

When Susan was a child, her abusive mother repeatedly told her she was stupid, ugly and never would succeed. When Susan did something wrong, her mother instructed everyone in the family not to speak to her. Only after she apologized could she participate in the family's activities. As a result, young Susan believed that she was loved and accepted only when she obeyed and was good.

Now that she has grown up and has her own family, Susan still has trouble looking people in the eye and believing that anyone wants to be her friend. When she attempts a new project, something inside her says, *It'll never work out; you'll fail for sure.* When she meets someone at church, she leaves as quickly as possible because, *They won't like me. No one would want to get to know me better.*

When Susan's children cry or have temper tantrums, she thinks, *See what a terrible mother I am? I can't even make my child happy.*

Laura, Susan's two-year-old, repeatedly has toilet training accidents, and Susan reacts in rage each time. In the back of her mind, she tells herself, *I know Laura can go potty in the toilet. She's not cooperating just to show me she hates me.*

Susan is believing the self-talk that was recorded in her brain during childhood. She'll never succeed, have close friendships, or control her outbursts until she begins to think differently about herself. She is fulfilling Proverbs 23:7: "For as he thinks within himself, so he is."

Our self-depreciating thoughts seem very reasonable and true at that moment. We may think, *I can't do anything right,* which seems valid, because we just made a mistake. But we fail to recall that the day before we succeeded in a very difficult project.

To break the grip of negative self-talk, we need to follow the instructions of Romans 12:3, 2 Corinthians 10:5 and Philippians 4:8.

First, we need to "think so as to have sound judgment" (Romans 12:3). God wants us to think truthfully about ourselves; to acknowledge our weaknesses and our strengths. Most of all, He wants us to believe we have value as His child and power through the Holy Spirit.

Therefore, we can think: *I will succeed in God's power. I am valuable as a human being, created by God. I can be a good friend, someone people like to be around.*

The *second* step in correcting negative self-talk is "taking every thought captive to the obedience of Christ" (2 Corinthians 10:5). If we think of our thoughts as darts that are thrown toward us, we realize that we have a choice whether or not to receive each thought. We have the power to take our thoughts captive, examine them, cast the thoughts away that do not honor God, and accept those that are godly and mature.

Many people become discouraged when an evil or improper thought enters their minds. They believe that they already have sinned. The truth is, we have not sinned until we allow our minds to dwell on the thought, when we say, "Yes, I'm going to think about this and claim it for my own."

We can choose to reject an ungodly thought or temptation before it becomes part of our thinking. While Jesus was in the wilderness, Satan tempted Him with ungodly thoughts, but He was without sin. The thoughts themselves were not sin; succumbing to them would have been. But Jesus did not sin; He rejected the unrighteous thoughts and replaced them with Scripture.

We can do the same in the *third* part of our process by using the guidelines for thinking given to us in Philippians 4:8: "fill your minds with those things that are good and that deserve praise: things that are true, noble, right, pure, lovely, and honorable" (GNB).

Thinking within those guidelines is a difficult, moment-by-moment process that requires breaking the habit of negative self-talk. No one can think, *O.K. I'm never going to say I hate myself again,* or *I'm never going to think I'm a bad mother again.*

It's not a one-time decision, but a growth process. It will take a long time to change the tape that is running in your mind. If, as a child, you repeatedly said to yourself "I'm no good," or "No one loves me," it's going to take extensive re-programming to wipe out all that negative information. *But it can be done!*

As we think soberly, take each thought captive and then determine if it fits into our guidelines, we'll correct our negative thinking. As a result,

INSTEAD OF THINKING	*WE'LL THINK:*
You dummy, look at what you did.	*I made a mistake, but it's not the end of the world.*

34

I can't do anything right.	*I didn't do as well this time, but next time I'll do better. I've learned something from this.*
If I don't hurry, I'm going to blow this whole thing.	*I'm not going to get anxious; I'll do my best and not rush.*
If I were a better mother, my child wouldn't act that way.	*My child isn't perfect, but I've done the best I know how.*
That's just like me. Everything I do turns out wrong.	*It's just like me to do the right thing, even if I make mistakes some time.*
You're never going to be perfect.	*Only Jesus is perfect. God just wants me to keep growing closer to Him.*
I hate myself.	*God loves me and I love myself. How can I not love something God made and loves?*
I'll never conquer this sin.	*It may be taking me awhile to get victory over this, but God knows I'll soon do it, in His power. He knows I'm in a process of growth, and He's patient with me.*
I'm so worried about. . . .	*God is in control. I'm going to trust Him.*

PROMPTERS FOR CHANGE

It *is* difficult to break the habit of negative self-talk, so we need prompters or signals to remind us to stop and notice how we've been thinking. For example, you might want to wear a rubber band around your wrist and "ping" yourself every time you allow something negative to take hold of your mind.

Also, pick one negative phrase that you seem to use often, and think of a positive phrase to replace it. Every time you think the belittling thought, reject it and focus on the positive one instead.

Another idea is to identify an external stimulus that can make you pay attention to what you've been thinking about yourself. For instance, every time you change the baby, think, "What have I been saying to myself in the last couple of minutes?" Or if you have a watch with an alarm, set it to go off every hour or half hour to remind you to examine your self-talk. Or every time your child asks for something to eat or drink, or when the phone rings, or the clock chimes . . . just choose something that happens regularly and frequently, and use it to help you correct any demeaning thoughts.

Soon you'll be able to share with others what Virginia shared with me: "During that summer and fall I had been telling myself over and over, day and night, 'You have ruined your life. You have ruined your children's lives. You fool. You idiot.' If I awoke in the night, those terrible thoughts were instantly in my mind and I could not get back to sleep. The counselor showed me that I was punishing myself and not forgiving myself for my past choices. I realized I could then choose to forgive myself and go on with life, or I could choose not to forgive myself and continue to punish myself and be miserable. It was very hard to choose to forgive myself; I felt I deserved to be punished. But I finally did forgive myself, and that horrible cracked record of punishment stopped, and it has not replayed since. Thank you, God."

WHAT YOU CAN DO

1. Make a list of all the things you feel guilty about. Read Psalm 103 and write down all the verses that relate to forgiveness. Ask God to forgive you for the things on your list, and forgive yourself. If possible, make right any wrongs you have done. Then, the next time you recall one of those incidents (self-talk), reject the thought by saying (out loud, if possible), "God has forgiven me. I've forgiven myself. I am cleansed. Praise the Lord!"

2. Pick one of the "promptings" for correcting self-talk and concentrate on it for a week.

Chapter 4

Child Abuse Causes Low Self-Image

No parent is perfect; fathers and mothers make mistakes, and some physically take out their anger and frustration on their children. Thus, those children's self-images are low, and their ability to effectively parent their own children is extremely diminished. This starts a tragic cycle. As a result, 60 percent of those interviewed by the self-help, crisis intervention organization, Parents Anonymous, report being abused as a child.

Beverly, a twenty-five-year-old woman, knows the child abuse, low self-image cycle. When she was a teenager, her stepfather, Lloyd, sexually abused her, and her mother told her she would never amount to anything good. Beverly later realized that her mother was jealous of her relationship with Lloyd.

Healing the Angry Heart

In a desperate attempt to flee the abuse, Beverly, at age sixteen, married Rich. But Rich couldn't keep a job. After two children were born, the stress of financial troubles, her own poor self-esteem and other pressures overwhelmed her at times, and she physically lashed out at her older son. Each time they moved and Rich tried to find a new job, Beverly vented her anger and tension by beating her son, because he resembled Rich in appearance and personality. She couldn't tell her mother or family about her problems. They had always said her marriage would fail.

Beverly eventually found the professional help she needed and dealt with her guilt from the incest. She learned to cope with the stress in her life and to recognize that she was displacing her anger from her husband onto her son. Rich still has trouble keeping a job, but Beverly is working part time. Through a support group and continued counseling, she is feeling better about herself. She is breaking the child abuse cycle.

The term *child abuse* strikes fear and guilt in many hearts; we realize that every person is capable of it. Most parents know the feeling of wanting to lash out, or of actually striking their child, and then looking over their shoulders, fearful that someone may have seen them. In the back of their minds, they may wonder, *Am I abusing my child?*

What is child abuse? People usually identify it with extreme forms of punishment. They may envision a parent holding a burning cigarette against young skin, or think of a man beating his girlfriend's son into unconsciousness and possibly death. Yet, Parents Anonymous lists six different types of abuse:

1. Physical abuse: any injury that is not accidental.
2. Physical neglect: lack of proper food, clothing, medical

care, parental guidance or supervision.

3. Sexual abuse: performing sexual acts with a child or knowing it is happening, but not taking action.

4. Verbal abuse: use of insulting, coarse or bad language, scolding harshly or reviling.

5. Emotional abuse: providing a negative emotional atmosphere, making the child feed inadequate, inferior or unimportant.

6. Emotional neglect: parent giving neither negative nor positive attention; not showing any feelings toward child.

The United States Congress defines child abuse as "the physical or mental injury, sexual abuse, negligent treatment or maltreatment of a child under the age of 18 by a person who is responsible for the child's welfare."

We don't often think of neglect, verbal lashings, or "putting a child down," as child abuse, but they are.

CAUSES OF CHILD ABUSE

Virtually all child abusers have low self-esteem and many have troubled marriages. They are generally socially isolated, with little support from their families, and they rarely get away from their children. They may resent the fact that another person's demands and care disrupts their own lives.

Child abusers tend to be depressed, lonely or fearful. They usually feel inadequate in the parenting role and know little about child development. Parents are more susceptible during a rapid series of change or crises. Also, many abusers are victims of a slight neurological impairment, which may not be detected by others, but which lowers their frustration tolerance.

Research shows that a child's crying is the behavior which most often instigates child abuse. The parent may interpret

41

the crying as, "You aren't meeting my needs—you are not a good parent." As a result, an insecure mother or father feels overwhelmed with frustration. This frustration is then translated into hostility, which is expressed in abusive behavior toward the one who appears to have caused it.

The second most common trigger of child abuse is toilet training.

The average age for abusive mothers is twenty-six. The majority of battered children are two years or younger.

Unfortunately, societal attitudes do not help child abusers. One detrimental attitude is that being a mother is no longer a valued profession. Public opinion subtly tells women they are wasting their time by being "just" housewives and homemakers. The hostile environment of such secular attitudes can generate frustration in mothers. They can be led to believe that others judge them as "a drain on society."

In addition, idealistic dreams about the "joys of motherhood" supply fuel for new mothers' expectations. Few mothers (or fathers) are prepared for the change in lifestyle that parenthood ushers in. They soon learn that, although being a parent is a joy, it also brings a hefty portion of physical and emotional exhaustion and tedium.

Another subtle influence on the problem of child abuse is our society's acceptance and approval of abortion. A parent may subconciously reason that if another person can legally kill a baby a few months before birth, what is so bad about roughing up a child a little afterward, especially if you don't kill him.

HELP AND HEALING

If you were abused in any way as a child, healing is available to you. You can break the cycle of child abuse that may have been passed down through your family for generations. Recognizing the causes of your low self-image can be the first step in your healing.

The first cause is that *your parent treated you as if you were unworthy of love or value.* So, of course, you would begin to believe that you didn't have value. Your self-talk as a child was most likely negative because your parents even may have told you that you weren't important, or a thousand other demeaning things. The way they treated you, whether it was actually abusive or simply neglectful, would cause you to think you had no worth or significance.

If this is your experience, I hope this section on self-image has been helpful and that you will begin to turn your thinking around to believe the truth: that you actually are very important and valuable. So valuable that God sent His most beloved Son, Jesus Christ, to die for your sins.

The second cause of your low self-esteem is that *as you were abused, you probably felt hate, anger and resentment toward your parent. But because you felt guilty for that reaction, you tried to repress those unpleasant feelings.* The guilt is still there, and that has made you think lowly of yourself.

"After all," an abused child may reason, "I shouldn't feel angry toward Mommy and Daddy. They are adults. They are supposed to know what they're doing. It must be my fault. If I didn't disobey, they wouldn't have to get angry at me. If I didn't attract Daddy, he wouldn't touch me in naughty places. It's wrong to hate them. Besides, doesn't Daddy buy me pretty things? He must love me. Doesn't Mommy tell me to get straight A's? She must love me. I'll do better and then they won't hurt me."

On and on the child rationalizes the parent's behavior because Mommy and Daddy are adults. Obviously, the child may not think this in so many words, but these often are the child's feelings.

One incest victim shared, "My dad couldn't be wrong; he was an adult. I decided I had been very bad and this was my punishment." Then, after a long pause, she continued, "I was just seven years old when I made that decision."

Unfortunately, the child is still angry, even though she tries to tell herself that she shouldn't be, and she represses it even more. She grows up, has her own children and wonders why she is uncontrollably angry and unnecessarily violent with them. Her anger stems from the guilt and repressed anger she experienced as a child.

If this is your struggle, first, *express your emotions in a constructive way.* Talk to God, and be honest. Tell Him that you feel angry for the way you were treated. You have every right to be angry, and you need to release those emotions. Repressed anger is detrimental to you physically and emotionally.

Be honest with God even if you're angry toward *Him* for allowing you to be abused. By telling Him your feelings, you can be free to accept His love. As you suffered during that time, He hurt with you. He did not desire for you to be abused.

Second, once you've expressed the anger from your past, *accept responsibility for the way you are reacting now.* Even though you are deeply angry at your parents, you cannot blame them for the way you treat your children. Instead, be accountable for your behavior and learn new responses. Apparently, you already are striving to do that, as you are reading this book.

Third, *seek professional Christian counseling.* Some psychologists believe that people may need to feel again the pain and hurt they experienced as children. In most cases, people cannot do that on their own, without a counselor's or psychologist's help. Ask God to guide you to a Christian professional who can help you. He will direct you; He wants you whole.

After she hit her toddler on several occasions, Amy found the help she needed from a counselor. After many years of therapy, she has dealt with the guilt that had built up during her teen years when she was sexually molested by her stepfather. She realizes now why she hated her body and felt dirty and unlovable, and finally is beginning to appreciate the wonderful framework God gave her.

Finally, *pray for your parents.* I don't mean pray in a revengeful way. Pray for their happiness, and that God will work in their lives. This is difficult, but you may find that it's hard to be bitter toward someone as you sincerely ask God to bless them. Bitterness and prayer cannot co-exist in a heart at the same moment. Praying for them will enable you to forgive them.

Also consider that, as they abused you, they didn't hate you, they hated themselves. They didn't know how to deal with the difficult aspects of their lives, and you were there to take the brunt of their frustration. They may even have been battered themselves as children.

Ruth discovered that was true of her abusing father. She struggled through life with a horrible self-image because of the physical and emotional abuse he had heaped upon her. She finally mustered up enough courage to ask him how he had been treated as a child. When he said he had been abused by his mother, she understood why he took out his frustration and self-hatred on her, and she forgave him.

Toward the end of her father's life, he wrote her many letters asking her if God would forgive him for the way he treated her. She always wrote back "yes." After he died, Ruth says, "My bottled up feelings toward him gradually drained away. The ugliness and sordidness evaporated under the sunshine of God's forgiveness through me toward him.

"Suddenly, I felt warmth and heavenly sorrow that he was gone and I couldn't tell him I loved him. But with it was a quiet joy and assurance that my father knows how I feel and how much I love him now."

Ruth thanks God for healing her painful memories and turning her life into one of forgiveness, praise and beauty.

WHAT YOU CAN DO

If you were abused or neglected as a child, forgive your parent and accept responsibility for your own actions. Pledge to pray for your parents every day.

Chapter 5
The Source of True Self-Esteem

This section about building self-esteem would be incomplete if I didn't tell you about the source of a true, good self-image. It is a relationship with God through His son, Jesus Christ.

Have you invited Jesus to come into your life and make you a child of God? I hope so. But if not, you can turn to Him right now and know that you have started a new life and are on your way to heaven.

The first step is to realize that we all are sinners. No matter how much goodness we see within ourselves, we still have sinned; we have done wrong things in disobedience to God's way. Everybody has! Romans 3:23 says: "Yes, all have sinned; all fall short of God's glorious ideal" (LB).

But the good news is that even though we have gone our

own way, apart from God, He still loves us very, very much. You've most likely heard John 3:16 before, but have you ever put your name into it and made it your own personal verse? Try it now, with my paraphrase: "For God loved _____ (your name) so much that He gave His only Son to die on the cross for _____'s sins, so that if _____ believes in Him, _____ shall not perish but have eternal life."

Second, we must realize that sin will cause us to die eternally, as Romans 6:23 explains: "For the wages of sin is death, but the free gift of God is eternal life in Jesus Christ our Lord" (LB).

We can't do anything about our sin, but Jesus can. In fact, He already has taken care of it. Romans 5:8 says, "But God showed His great love for us by sending Christ to die for us while we were still sinners" (LB).

We never can be good enough to deserve eternal life, so instead, God offers it to us as a free gift. "Because of His kindness you have been saved through trusting Christ. And even trusting is not of yourselves; it too is a gift from God. Salvation is not a reward for the good we have done, so none of us can take any credit for it" (Ephesians 2:8,9, LB).

Yet, just as a birthday gift is not yours until you unwrap it and take it for your own, this free gift of salvation is not yours until you accept it and believe God has given it to you. John 1:12,13 (LB) promises, "But to all who receive Him, He gave the right to become children of God. All they needed to do was to trust Him to save them. All those who believe this are reborn! Not a physical rebirth resulting from human passion or plan—but from the will of God."

If you desire to know Christ, I suggest that you pray something like this: "Heavenly Father, thank You for sending Jesus to die on the cross for my sins. I realize that I have lived apart from You, but now I want Jesus, through your Holy Spirit, to come into my life, cleanse me of my sin and take control of my life. From this point on, I give myself to You so that You can work Your plan in me. In Jesus name, amen."

You can be sure that Jesus came into your life when you asked Him, and He wants you to have that assurance. He promised to come into our lives, and He always keeps His promises. "So whoever has God's Son has life; whoever does not have His Son does not have life. I have written this to you who believe in the Son of God so that you *know* you have eternal life" (1 John 5:12,13, LB. Italics are mine.)

If you prayed that prayer, 2 Corinthians 5:17 says you are now a new person: "When someone becomes a Christian he becomes a brand new person inside. He is not the same any more. A new life has begun!"

As a result, you are a child of God. Think of it: a son or a daughter of the Lord of heaven and earth. That is where good self-image comes from. Being a child of God can give us security and love, if we grow in Christ. And we grow by learning more about the Christian life and by applying what we learn.

If you became a Christian by reading this chapter, please write me so that I can encourage you in your new faith. (You'll find my address at the end of this book.) And be sure to find a church where you can meet with other Christians and find out more about your life in Christ.

Section II

Take Anger
Out of Danger

Chapter 6
Examining Anger

Anger.
Anger!
ANGER!
Why did God give humans this strong emotion anyway?
Didn't He know it would get us into a lot of trouble?

The primary reason we have the ability to get angry is
because God made us in His image, and He gets angry!

The second reason is that it helps us survive. Anger, as all
emotions, generates energy. In the case of anger, that energy
gives us extra motivation to struggle to live. What is anger?
Dr. H. Norman Wright defines it as a "strong emotion of
displeasure."[1] In my workshops about anger, mothers have
defined it as rage, a blazing flame, intense frustration, violent
wrath and other anguished feelings. Although anger has many

basic causes, such as being misunderstood and having one's feelings hurt, over 95 percent of these mothers attributed theirs to frustration. Such frustration may stem from having a goal or desire blocked, not getting enough done, facing deadlines, or a host of other problems.

Sometimes, rather than honestly sharing our anger, we hide it behind other reactions and don't recognize it for what it is. We might say we're aggravated, upset, cross or annoyed. Somehow those words don't sound as bad as "angry." We try to disguise it because many people, especially Christians, mistakenly believe that anger is always sinful. Those people usually equate anger with "losing control," and thus brand all anger as wrong. But people *do* get angry *without* losing control and that's not wrong.

THE DIFFERENCE BETWEEN FEELINGS AND ATTITUDES

My generation grew up thinking we weren't supposed to be angry. Anger was an unpleasant emotion that wasn't acceptable in public; it wasn't respectable. So I, like many others, tried to push my angry feelings back down inside of me.

It wasn't until a few years ago that I learned the difference between feeling anger and having an attitude of anger. *A feeling is that first flash of emotion within us, over which we have no control.* It wells up within us before we even realize it's there. For instance, if your best friend came up to you and hit you in the face, you most likely would feel angry! No matter why he or she did that, you still will react emotionally. That is a feeling.

Our first flash feelings, our emotions, were built into us by God and are neither right nor wrong. They have no morality in themselves, because they are not something we can control. Some of our emotions are pleasant, such as happiness, joy or calmness, and some are unpleasant, such as anger, fear, sadness and irritation, but they are not right or wrong.

An attitude is what we decide to do with a feeling once it emerges. It involves a conscious choice, which leads to our actions. We usually don't have too much trouble letting pleasant feelings turn into proper attitudes. That's easy. Feeling happy can become an attitude of cheerfulness, joy or generosity. But with an unpleasant feeling, we have a more difficult choice of whether to turn it into a godly or unrighteous attitude.

Here's another way to clarify this difference:

A FEELING	AN ATTITUDE
has no morality	is moral
is an unconscious spontaneous reaction	is a conscious choice
is an emotion given to us by God	is a decision I make about what I will do with my feeling
is pleasant or unpleasant	is right or wrong

That's a general explanation; now let's focus on handling anger. Once we experience that first flash of anger, we can choose to let it turn into an ungodly attitude of bitterness, resentment or hate, or into an attitude of love, forgiveness and trusting God.

If we consistently choose to allow angry feelings to become angry attitudes, we quickly get caught in a habit or pattern of anger. The more we travel this downward spiral, the harder it is to choose godly reactions of love.

Healing the Angry Heart

This same point is made in Ephesians 4:26,27: "If you are angry, don't sin by nursing your grudge. Don't let the sun go down with you still angry—get over it quickly; for when you are angry you give a mighty foothold to the devil" (LB).

This verse acknowledges that we are going to get angry (and it's not wrong), and then tells us we should not let that anger become sin—let it turn into an attitude—by neglecting to deal with it. We should not ignore it or say we don't feel angry.

Paul writes, ". . . don't sin by nursing your grudge," which tells us anger can become sin if we let it continue without dealing with it. It's as if we allow ourselves to enjoy being angry. Isn't it true that anger sometimes feels good when we decide to wallow in it?

Instead, God wants us to deal with it quickly, not let it eat away inside of us. "Don't let the sun go down with you still angry," verse 26 directs. What a good guideline! Our angry feeling wouldn't have time to turn into a negative attitude or habit if we followed that command. If we all resolved our anger before sunset, we wouldn't go to bed angry with our spouses or wake up and lash out at our children. We wouldn't give our anger a chance to turn into bitterness or resentment . . . and an ulcer.

Christian psychologist David Augsburger explains it this way: "Anger is a vital, valid, natural emotion. As an emotion, it is in itself neither right nor wrong. The rightness or wrongness depends on the way it is released and exercised."[2]

Why is it necessary and important to understand the difference between feelings and attitudes? Because if we believe all anger is sinful, as soon as we feel angry, we think we've sinned. Then we condemn ourselves and try to squelch the feeling. We tell ourselves we aren't really angry because it's wrong to feel that way. As a result, we become even more angry. As one young mother said, "I get angry with myself for being angry!"

When we condemn ourselves for feeling angry (something we can't prevent in the first place), we push it deep within us, where it builds up with anger from other situations. We think ignoring it will cause it to go away. In reality, when we bury anger *alive,* it boils inside of us until we release it in an emotional outburst. Then we wonder where all that anger came from.

If we would instead recognize our feelings of anger for what they are, part of our humanness, and not try to shove them away, we could deal with them effectively. By realizing that the *feelings of anger* are not sin, we can accept ourselves as we truly are, human beings with feelings; and then we can control our anger.

Dr. Theodore Isaac Rubin says, ". . . our feelings control us when we subvert them and are no longer aware they exist. They then have an autonomy of their own. When we know what we feel, when our feelings are integrated as parts of the whole of us, then regardless of their intensity, we remain completely in charge of ourselves and of all our feelings—as part of a central autonomy.

"Acceptance, real acceptance of angry feelings, without harsh judgment or moral equivocation, combined with the *ability* to express the anger, will then make possible a choice regarding its expression."[3]

THREE REACTIONS TO ANGER

Sharon, a twenty-eight-year-old mother of preschoolers, grew up in a Christian home. Her father was a minister and often told Sharon, who was strong-willed: "It's wrong to be angry." "Control yourself, some of our congregation might hear you." Or, "Only God can have righteous anger."

She matured into adulthood trying to squelch every feeling of anger and condemning herself when she experienced "unspiritual" emotions. When one of her children disobeyed early in a day, she crammed down inside her the feeling of anger. As the day progressed, more childish disobedience and other problems and pressures caused her to push more and more anger below the surface. By the end of the day, she felt like a volcano ready to erupt. Often, she exploded when something upsetting occurred in the evening, such as her husband being late for dinner.

Sharon asked for help from a Christian friend who is a psychologist. When he explained the difference between the feeling and attitude of anger, she had difficulty believing he was correct. But when he showed her Ephesians 4:26,27, she had to agree with him.

Then he explained to her that when she feels angry, she has a choice of three reactions. She can deny, direct or declare her anger.

Denying our anger is the most destructive choice you or I can make when we feel that first flash of anger. Sharon learned that the hard way. Denying means that we refuse to accept that we're angry. It's when we say: "Who, me? Angry? I am not! I NEVER GET ANGRY!"

The truth is, everyone gets angry at some point in time, but most people don't know how to express it healthfully. Unfortunately, as John Powell says, "When I repress my emotions, my stomach keeps score."[4]

When we deny anger, we bottle it up inside of us. Then, at an inappropriate time, we explode, spraying the shattered glass of anger all around us, injuring our relationships with others. That is what Sharon experienced. Fortunately, she is beginning to accept her feelings of anger. As a result, she can control herself more often.

Obviously, as Sharon learned, denial is not a healthy, or godly, way to deal with anger. As Dr. H. Norman Wright says, "Getting angry is not necessarily a sin, but repression of anger is always a sin."[5]

Our second choice is *directing our anger*. This means we are aware of our anger and we try to control it by doing something physical. At the beginning of this chapter, we said that anger generates energy. If you've never noticed this energy, the next time you're angry, take note of whether or not your body is physically tense and keyed up. Many women have told me that when they are angry, they want to hit or throw or bang something. That's energy!

When we direct our anger, we realize we're angry and then direct the resulting energy. Maybe we scrub the floor or furiously push the vacuum back and forth. Directing it can be good in itself but unless we discover the real reason for our anger and deal with it, we will not solve the underlying problem, and the anger will return. Therefore, the best way to respond to our anger is to combine directing it with the third choice: *declaring our anger*.

Declaring our anger means communicating our feelings in such a way that the other people involved can receive and accept them. If we rant and rave, accuse and blame, then we'll only make others uncooperative and angry, even if we feel better. By declaring our anger in a healthy way, we'll be in control and influence others positively. In chapter 9, we'll talk more about declaring our anger through a four-step process.

In the next chapter, we will examine some causes of our anger. In the meantime, whenever you feel that first flash of

Healing the Angry Heart

anger, stop and consider how you will react. Will you deny, direct or declare?

WHAT YOU CAN DO

1. Identify in which of the three basic ways—denying, directing, or declaring—you react to anger most often.
2. Learn what your anger feels like when you first experience it.

Chapter 7
Causes of Anger

The next aspect in our search for controlling anger is discovering its causes. Each one of us probably could name a myriad of reasons for becoming angry and, of course, this book addresses many in other chapters: poor self-esteem, inability to cope with stress, ineffective discipline of chil–dren, etc. But in this chapter, we'll focus on three others: displacement, our husbands and unrealistic expectations.

DISPLACEMENT

Elizabeth and her two-year-old daughter are in Judy's home, visiting with Judy and her three-year-old son. Eliza-beth and Judy are talking as the children play on the floor. Elizabeth's daughter continually yanks Judy's son's toys away and makes him cry. Elizabeth tells her to share. Again and again the little girl yanks the toys away and Elizabeth becomes more and more embarrassed. She speculates, "I bet Judy thinks I'm a terrible mother." Elizabeth continues to try to help her daughter play cooperatively, but nothing works. As she worries about Judy's possible critical thoughts, she becomes more and more upset. Finally, in a burst of exasperation, Elizabeth grabs her daughter by the arm, slaps her bottom hard and reprimands her, saying, "You start sharing right now or we're going home." Looking away from Judy's startled glance, she blushes in embarrassment and tries to distract her crying daughter with a toy.

This scene is an example of displacement. *Displacement is the transference of an emotion to an object which is logically inappropriate.*

Did you notice how Elizabeth transferred her embarrassment into anger at her daughter?

As I look back to when I was reacting uncontrollably toward Darcy, I can see how I displaced my feelings. I usually was irritated or angry with Larry or myself, but because I couldn't manage that situation, I leveled my frustration against an innocent bystander, Darcy. She usually had not done anything to deserve my blow-up; she was just the nearest object that couldn't strike back.

I usually blamed Darcy for my outbursts, thinking her disobedience caused my anger. Now I know it was only the straw that broke the back of my patience. Other situations and relationships were at play, but I didn't see their influence or significance.

If we can begin to see when we displace our anger from the real cause to our children, we'll be on our way to learning godly reactions to their disobedience. The best way to prevent displacement is to deal with each situation or problem as it occurs, instead of storing them up. Also, by recognizing when we are about to displace anger, we can stop ourselves from spilling out frustrations over other problems onto our children's misbehavior.

Now, let's go back to Elizabeth and revise that scene.

As Elizabeth and Judy talk, the children play on the floor. Elizabeth's daughter continually yanks the little boy's toys away, making him cry. Disconcerted with her daughter's behavior, Elizabeth comments to Judy, "I feel so embarrassed when my little girl doesn't share. I just don't know what to do about it."

"Oh, don't worry about it," Judy responds. "It's perfectly normal for a two-year-old not to share. My son has learned to share only in the last couple of weeks."

"Oh, really? Well, I guess she'll learn someday, too!" Elizabeth breathes a sigh of relief and settles into the sofa to enjoy the visit.

Of course, not every situation will turn out perfect just because we share our feelings. But by recognizing those feelings and trying to deal with them, we can prevent displacement. Even if we cannot change our situation, we still will release the pressure that is building inside us.

Dr. Rubin puts it this way: "Big blow-ups are really accumulated results of repressed potential small air-cleaning blow-ups."

Cora shared with me that one evening she felt angry about having to do the dishes while her two sons and husband relaxed watching television. Instead of continuing to dwell on it, she stood near them and screamed at the top of her voice. After they jumped in fright, and she explained why she yelled, they continued to watch television and she finished the dishes—laughing and happy. She says that if she hadn't done that right then, she most likely would have stewed about it all night and taken out her pent-up anger on her little boy the next day.

I hope you won't have to scream and scare everyone (instead, ask your family to help you with the dishes), but I do hope you'll communicate and declare your feelings as soon as they occur. Then you won't displace them onto someone else.

YOUR HUSBAND

For several months, Sarah shared with me her struggles about anger. Whenever I related how God had healed my relationship with Larry, Sarah always insisted that there was no disunity between her and her husband. As time passed, though, she began to feel freer to tell me about their disagreements and problems. Yet she believed her problems were never caused by his inadequacies—because he said they weren't!

When I said I thought he had some weaknesses, she seemed surprised. It was very difficult for her to realize that his reactions contributed to her anger problem.

When my temper was out of control, I was not like Sarah. I was only too eager to see my husband's flaws. The more I dwelled upon his failings, the more dissatisfied and unhappy I became, with him and with life. It wasn't until I began to feel better about myself that I stopped trying to change Larry. Then God changed him.

I had to accept the fact that I wasn't perfect and neither was Larry. Just as I was dissatisfied with some of his characteristics and actions, so he was unhappy with elements of my life. We had to accept each other at our levels of maturity. Every relationship is imperfect, because everybody has flaws. But, praise the Lord, God isn't finished with us yet!

He can do a much better job of changing our spouses than we can. He runs a successful business changing lives—He's very good at it. He knows our mates inside out, their every thought and motivation, while we can only guess and wonder. I know; I tried to figure Larry out for many years. Just when I thought I had done it, I discovered I was wrong!

In fact, our interference hampers God. When I first heard that, I thought, "Humphf! Well, excuse me! I was only trying to help." Unfortunately, our "help" is not help at all. It's a hindrance. God can—and wants to—do it alone. But He does delegate to us an important job: to love and accept our spouse! Then, He'll do whatever else is necessary.

Because God wants us to have happy marriages, we can trust Him to do what is best, and we can love our husbands by faith. Proverbs 3:4-6 says: "If you want favor with both God and man (our mates), and a reputation for good judgment and common sense, then trust the Lord completely; don't ever trust yourself. In everything you do, put God first, and He will direct you and crown your efforts with success [a happy, godly marriage]" (LB).

As we allow God to work in our marriages, it is comforting to remember that we most often get angry with the people who mean the most to us. Sharing our angry *feelings*, not attitudes or actions, reflects that love. It tells our spouse, "I respect you enough to want to share this part of myself with you. Doing this shows my commitment to our relationship." But we need to be careful to share with "I feel" messages, rather than saying "you are . . ." or "you make me . . ."

Watching the Lord work in my husband's life (and mine) sometimes made me think, "Lord, you don't know what you're doing. That'll never get him to come around." But God performed miracles, and now I'm content with our beautiful, rich life together.

I strongly believe in the principle of allowing God to work

in our husband's lives, but that doesn't mean I think we're doormats to be walked on. Submission means "to submit," and we are to submit to our husbands who we are, what we believe, what we'd like, etc. Then we can leave the results to the Lord.

Luci was angry with her husband about his unhappiness with the small apartment in which their family of six lived. She explains, "He's the major cause of my discomfort. He's so disillusioned that he is incapable of giving me any encouragement. He's so tired of our apartment that he stays away from here as much as possible, which isn't very much fun for me. I try to do my best, but it doesn't seem to be good enough. I'm feeling angry because of his feelings toward our outgrown abode."

Luci gathered her courage together and shared her feelings with her husband. She filled me in: "We talked a bit and he reassured me that his disappointment is not a reflection on me as a homemaker, but rather a reflection of our financial pressures."

She had shared her feelings; she had submitted who she was at that moment, and she felt better because of it. The financial problems weren't gone, but she wouldn't take her tension and anger out on her children.

Another cause of anger is the problem of taking responsibility *for* our husbands. I am not responsible for Larry's reactions or behavior. I am responsible *to* him, in the sense that I need to be the wife that God wants me to be. But I am not accountable to Larry.

My friend Sandy shared with me that she and her husband traveled into Los Angeles one day to take their kids to the zoo. After spending the day there, they left a little later than they'd wanted and were stuck in traffic on the way home. Sandy started feeling tense, afraid that her husband would be angry. Then she realized that she was taking responsibility *for* her husband's reaction. She consciously relaxed and decided she couldn't change his attitude even if he were upset (which, it turned out, he wasn't). Sandy's choice showed her growing self-esteem.

UNREALISTIC EXPECTATIONS

As we have said, our husbands aren't perfect. Neither are our kids. At times, we are not displacing—they are the direct causes of our anger. Let's look into some of those situations.

One of the main reasons our children make us angry is that we have unrealistic expectations of their behavior. We believe they can do or understand something, but they can't. Then when they disobey or misbehave, we get angry.

That's what happened to a young mother I recently observed in a department store. Her six- or seven-year-old daughter had begged to push the stroller that held her one-year-old brother. The mother finally relented and, as the little girl followed her mother, trying to maneuver the stroller between the racks of clothes, the stroller tipped over. Her mother turned and saw her daughter straining with all her might to stand it back up again. The woman immediately righted the stroller and, with a fierce scowl, yelled at the little girl, "Now, look what you've done." She instantly smacked her daughter's bottom. Tears sprang into the little girl's eyes, and she hung her head in fear and humiliation.

Similar circumstances happen many times a day across America. The situations are different, but the underlying cause is the same: an over-stressed mother expects too much from her child. When the child fails or doesn't meet the parent's expectations, the parent becomes angry and over-reacts.

Healing the Angry Heart

Please don't think I'm condemning that mother. I've been in her shoes. She most likely had a to-do list a mile long, wanted to get a gift quickly in the store, and had listened all day to her daughter's constant chattering. When the stroller tipped over, it was just too much. She had reached her frustration level, and she believed that her daughter had pushed the stroller over on purpose.

In situations like this, we expect a child to do something that he is not physically or emotionally ready to handle. He's not there yet in his development. That mother in the store wasn't wrong to allow her daughter to push the stroller, but when it tipped over, she could have thought, "Well, that stroller is a lot for her to handle. My getting upset is not going to make her stronger."

We also create problems when we compare children. I've often felt uptight because someone else's child could do something that Darcy couldn't—at the same age. Then I take into account the individual differences, personalities and temperaments of each unique child. This helps balance my perspective.

This is a prime area where parents lack training. Most of the time we don't know what to expect or we are uninformed about the developmental patterns of our children. We expect too much, are disappointed and react in anger and frustration.

Instead, every parent can take advantage of the many books available that outline the approximate ages at which children can do things. If you can't afford to buy one, the library has many. The government also offers pamphlets on child development. But don't forget that every child has his own developmental schedule and may not exactly follow the "text book" cases.

If you think you might be expecting too much from your

child and are getting angry as a result, refer to a child development book and make a list of the things you can expect from your child at his age. Affix the list to your refrigerator. Then, when your child does something that is listed, before dealing with the child, walk to the refrigerator, make a check mark by that action, and realize that your child is only doing what is normal for his age level. Does he spill his milk at every meal? Check it off. Does he scribble on the walls? Check it off. Does he mess up his room with toys and have difficulty putting them away? Check it off.

After you've checked off his behavior and you realize that it can be expected, you can go back to the child and discipline him calmly and effectively.

Many times, a child displeases his parent because he's going through a "phase." Maybe he says "no" to everything, or stutters, or wants to do everything himself. Once the parent understands that the child will grow out of it, he can relax and not get so upset. Quite often, the sooner the parent accepts it, the sooner it goes away.

Once when Darcy was a baby, I stood in line to get her picture taken. I was chatting with two sisters, both of whom had toddlers around two years old. We were talking about the different phases children go through, and one sister commented that her daughter was going through a "cussing" phase. Her sister looked astonished at her and said, "She wouldn't cuss if you didn't."

How true! Often our actions influence our children's behavior, and then we get angry at them for acting that way!

We might become angry because our child is mirroring a bad habit of ours—and we don't want to be reminded that we have it. God uses children to mature us, and when they start acting like we do, we feel put down a notch. Sometimes, we don't even realize why we're so upset with them, but it's because they're doing what God has been telling us not to do. For example, Darcy's whining often aggravates me, and then I remember that I complain to God about my circumstances.

Another cause of anger is that we expect our children to be well-behaved when they're too tired to be. I've often regretted trying to fit my children into my schedule. At times I've continued shopping, knowing my children were getting too tired or too hungry to go on. Then my communication became battle cries of "Stop whining," "We'll be home for lunch in a few minutes," "Stop poking your brother," and "Get off the floor!" Whatever few, harried minutes of shopping I gained by continuing with my plans, I paid for with irritation and anger.

I also have regretted expecting my children to ignore all the "no-no's" in my home when their curiosity overrides their self-control. As a result, I gave in and child-proofed my home. They have enough temptations, which cannot be put away, to teach them self-control, without deliberately leaving objects that could be removed. Why tempt our power to control ourselves when Junior breaks our family heirlooms? In the future, we will have plenty of time to display our favorite knickknacks.

Children need a safe place to play where they can have fun and expend their energy without fear of discipline for knocking over furniture. If you live in an apartment and don't have a yard, make a point to go to a park or even walk a couple of blocks so that your child can vent his God-given energy. Being cooped up isn't good for him—or you!

I love to tell the story about the father and his toddler daughter who were walking through a national forest. The father instructed his daughter, "Stay on the path, honey." But she continually ran back and forth, hither and yon, noticing every tree, bird and flower. Several times he told her to stay on the path and each time he became increasingly irritated. Finally, he grabbed her arm and said through gritted teeth, "I said stay on the path." She looked up at him in wide-eyed amazement and asked, "What's a path, Daddy?"

Our expectations of our children must take into account that they don't have the same knowledge we do. Sometimes they don't know what a path is, or how to make the bed, or what is involved in cleaning the bathroom.

Consider for a moment what it must be like to be a child and have adults telling you what to do, but you don't understand what a word means or how to do what they want. They must feel as I would if a computer expert set a personal computer in front of me and said, "Load this disk into the computer's memory."

Having never seen a computer before, I ask, "How do you do it?"

"Well, it's very simple," he replies. "You just do it."

In the computer expert's brain, a procedure as simple as loading a disk is a one-step process. But for me, it's a multi-faceted procedure, because I don't know where to start.

Sometimes your child doesn't know where to start. You may tell him to make the bed, something you've done for many years. Obviously, it's a simple task. But not for him. Therefore you have to break it down into steps: "First, you take off the pillow. Then pull back the sheet and blanket. Now smooth the bottom sheet . . ." etc.

If we could look at our interaction with our child through his eyes, we quickly would see when our expectations are too high and become overwhelming for him.

Let's be realistic in what we want and not be like the mother

Healing the Angry Heart

who gazed down at her child, who was screaming and kicking on the grocery store floor. She angrily muttered to an older woman passing by, "Look at him. It's disgusting. He's acting just like a two-year-old!"

The woman whispered, "How old is he?"

The mother looked amazed at first. Then her face relaxed and she started to grin. "I forgot. He *is* a two-year-old!"

WHAT YOU CAN DO

1. Evaluate your anger toward your child and determine if most of it is a result of displacement. If it is not, identify the real cause.

2. To discover what unrealistic expectations you have of your child, purchase, or check out of the library, a book about child development.

Chapter 8
Defusing Anger

Now that we've examined anger and some of its causes, let's look at a constructive method of defusing our anger. By going through the following four-step process every time we get angry, we can have healthy reactions. *Healthy* means being fully aware of and possessing our feelings (as opposed to our feelings possessing and controlling us).

The four-step process is:

1. Realize we feel angry.
2. Magnetize our minds away from our anger by using a distractor.
3. Recognize the underlying cause of our anger.
4. Verbalize our anger appropriately.

1. REALIZE ANGRY FEELINGS

Elaine has been a Christian for four years and condemns

herself for the way she reacts toward her five-year-old son. When I asked her to describe her anger, she used strong terms, such as "rage," "heat," "out of control." Then I asked her how she feels before she loses her temper. She replied, "I feel calm, and then I suddenly blow up."

I explained to her that she had repressed and ignored her first feelings of anger for so long, that she no longer believed they existed. I instructed her to begin paying attention to early warning signals before she blew up and to realize she feels angry.

Recognizing early warning signs of anger—your "red-flag warnings"—gives you time to deal with your feelings before they become destructive. To discover these signals, write down facts about the last three times you blew it. Then recall how you felt fifteen minutes, ten minutes and five minutes before the flare-ups. If you can't remember those details, then monitor the next three times it happens.

Chances are, you'll see a pattern of warnings in the three incidents. For instance, fifteen minutes before I blow up, I usually am worried about a time schedule or some other pressure. At the ten-minute warning, I feel tense and hurried. Even though, on the outside, I may not look hassled, inside I feel like the wheels are turning faster than normal. My five-minute signal is that I'm gritting and grinding my teeth and raising my voice in quick, terse commands.

When you become aware of your own unique red-flag warnings, you can realize that your fifteen-minute countdown has started. Then you can break the cycle by using a "distractor," which is part of the second step.

2. MAGNETIZE YOURSELF AWAY FROM ANGER

The second step is to magnetize your mind away from your anger by using what is called a distractor. A distractor is anything you can use to take your mind off your anger, if only for a few minutes. This gives you a break to cool down. Anger always causes physical tension and energy, but a distractor helps to relieve that tension before you blow up at another person.

Being distracted for a few minutes allows us to come back to the situation with an improved, calmer perspective. Like the whistling kettle, the steam of our anger is released. The cause of the anger is still there (that's taken care of in step three), but at least the energy that makes us want to lash out is gone.

Here are a few possible distractors:

Take a vigorous walk.

Run in place.

Hit a pillow or a punching bag.

Take a shower (with or without screaming).

Sing loudly.

Take ten slow, deep breaths; count them loud.

Play a musical instrument.

Recite an uplifting Bible verse.

Telephone a friend, a hotline or a professional counselor.

The important part of this exercise is to determine our distracting action beforehand (while we are calm), practice it, and ask God to remind us to use it when we start the fifteen-minute countdown.

For instance, during a peaceful period, I tell myself that the next time I feel angry, I'll take three steps backward and walk away from the irritating or frustrating situation. I continue to remind myself and rehearse it in my mind. I may even take three steps backward once in a while to practice. Then, when I notice I'm getting within that fifteen- or ten-minute count-down range, I remember, "Aha! It's time for me to take three steps backward and walk away!" That gives me time to think through what's causing my anger and how I can resolve it.

Deep breathing is another simple distractor that I have found helpful. It is especially effective, because intense emotions inhibit breathing. As I get angry my chest muscles seem to tighten and tense up, but slow, deep breathing eliminates that pressure.

After we distract ourselves and cool down, we can go on to the third step.

3. RECOGNIZE THE CAUSE OF OUR ANGER

The third step is to recognize the underlying cause of your anger. In most cases, the immediate circumstances are not the cause of anger. Instead, we displace our anger from the real cause. Remember displacement? That's the transference of an emotion to a logically inappropriate object.

I find it helpful to keep a mental checklist of possible causes, which I quickly go through to try to determine the actual cause. Here are some questions for you to consider:

Physical: Am I tired? Do I need some exercise? Have I been eating too much sugar? Am I in a premenstrual depression?

Psychological: Am I thinking negatively about something? Am I worried? Is a relationship troubling me? Are my expectations for myself unrealistic? Am I feeling embarrassed, frustrated or insecure about something? Is my self-esteem low? Have my goals or desires been blocked? Has my child mirrored a bad habit of mine?

Spiritual: Am I not trusting God? Do I have some unconfessed sin? Is there someone I need to forgive? Am I bitter toward someone or God?

It is important to dig up the underlying cause and expose it. Then we can recognize that whatever is going wrong probably doesn't warrant the kind of intense reaction and behavior that's building within us.

Once you identify the true cause, you can move onto the fourth and final step.

4. VERBALIZE ANGER

The last step is to verbalize your anger appropriately. This means using "I" messages instead of "you" messages. "I" messages express how you feel or what your opinion is, without telling the other person what to do about it (unless he or she asks). "I" messages express your needs.

"You" messages express blame, as in, "You make me angry," "You shouldn't do that," etc.

In addition to watching the wording, we need to monitor our motives. We should not use "I" messages to try to subtly change the other person. Instead, we should honestly share our feelings, while trusting God to control our circumstances.

We also can verbalize our anger by calling a friend who will keep a confidence and not put us down for our emotions. Another possibility is to call a hot line, a professional counselor or our pastor.

It is most effective to express our feelings at the time of the misunderstanding. If we can't seem to talk about them at that moment, though, we can prepare ourselves for verbalizing them later by writing them out in a speech. A woman shared this insight with me and says it works for her. When she realizes that she is angry with someone, whether it is her husband, a neighbor or a friend, she first determines what really is bothering her, and then she writes it down. By doing so, she can ensure that she expresses her feelings in a way the other person can accept. Then she reads it to someone else who can help her critique it. Finally, she practices it before she actually calls or visits the person involved.

Healing the Angry Heart

This process gives her the courage she needs to confront the person, because she knows she's expressing herself in the best possible way. If the other person rejects her feelings, she doesn't experience guilt because she did the best she could. She tells herself that if that person won't accept her opinions, maybe he or she is not a true friend after all.

In expressing feelings, we should be "speaking the truth in a spirit of love" (Ephesians 4:15, GNB). That begins with being responsible for my reactions. No one makes me be angry; it is my choice.

Once I am accountable for my own response, I need to express my feelings appropriately and ask forgiveness for my part of the problem. Whether or not the other person accepts my apology or changes his mind or actions, I can choose healthy reactions and not try to control the other person. I can trust God to work in both of our lives.

Recently I applied these principles when a woman broke a promise to me and I felt deeply hurt. After the hurt came the anger, and I knew I would have to travel through my four-step process so that I wouldn't take my anger out on my children.

I realized that I was indeed angry. Even after I tried to understand my friend's viewpoint, I still believed that she had treated me inappropriately.

Then I played the piano for a while to pound out some of the energy that my anger was creating. That was my distractor.

The third step, finding the real cause of my anger, was obvious. Yet, when I thought more about the situation, I discovered even more reasons why I was angry. For instance, her broken promise prevented me from completing a project I'd promised for someone else. Therefore, not only was I angry because of how she had treated me, but because it influenced my reputation before others.

78

Finally, I verbalized my anger in a letter to her. I really let my fury fly; then I edited it to make my sharing appropriate and acceptable. In the letter, I asked her to forgive me for my reactions and I shared how she had hurt me. Larry read my edited letter and approved it.

As I typed the final letter, I decided to wait one week before I mailed it, to make sure that the Lord wanted me to send it.

The next day, my anger was gone. I knew I wouldn't mail that letter. "Verbalizing" my anger, even on paper, had dissolved it, and I was able to forgive her. Today I have no bitterness toward her and the letter sits in my file as a testimony to God's grace.

WHAT YOU CAN DO

1. Every time you get angry, follow the four-step process: realize, magnetize, recognize and then verbalize.

2. Write down which distractor you will use and then practice it.

Section III
Don't Let Stress Become Distress

Chapter 9
Expectations of Perfection

My friend, Norma, knows about stress. Her husband left her and their two young sons for another woman, and he refuses to pay any support. Then Norma was evicted from her apartment, because the owner found out her salary had been cut in half. He was afraid she'd have trouble paying the rent. That same landlord would not fix her mailbox, so she had to go to the post office for all her mail. Her husband ran up large bills on their credit cards, and since he didn't have a checking account (he puts his money into his girlfriend's account), the creditors took all of the money from Norma's checking account and her sons' savings accounts.

Norma continues to look for a new job, but in the meantime, she cannot collect welfare. The government says her husband should be paying her $200 a month for support, which puts her earnings over the limit for welfare. But, of course, he's not paying, so she's without help.

The afternoon she came to see me and do her laundry, we had a nice visit. When she went out to her car to load up the clean laundry, she found her front tire flat. We opened the trunk to put on the spare and found it flat, too. Her husband had not told her that he hit the rim of the spare when he borrowed the car.

Talk about stress! This woman knows what it is. But she also knows how to spell relief: J . . . e . . . s . . . u . . . s.

Listen to what she says about her ordeal: "Even though I don't like what's happening to me, I know that it has to happen. Because, to tell you the truth, I've never had to grow up before. This is forcing me to grow up. And in the meantime, my relationship with the Lord is growing like it never has before. Somehow He's meeting my needs; not my wants, but He *is* providing for my needs. In fact, I've received checks in the mail from total strangers. At Christmas time, someone gave me money to buy the kids' presents, and someone gave us a Christmas tree. It just goes on and on like that. One time I prayed, 'Lord stop doing so much for me. I just can't handle it!' I know that sounds weird but I couldn't accept so many good things happening.

"All I can say is, sometimes I thank the Lord for all this stress in my life, even though I want it to end today. I'm growing and changing. He's showing me He loves me. I've never sensed that love so deeply before."

Your stresses may be greater than the ones in Norma's life, or they may be less. But everyone experiences stress. In this section, we will talk about how we can keep stress from becoming distress. We'll identify some stress producers and godly reactions. Let's start off by defining stress.

DEFINING STRESS

Stress is any condition or situation that imposes upon us demands for change. It can begin with internal or environmental forces, and it usually reveals itself in physical or mental/emotional tension. The dictionary says, "Stress is any force exerted upon a body that tends to strain or deform its shape."

That's how stress feels, isn't it? It strains us; it tries to deform our shape. In Christians, stress tries to push faith and trust out of our "shape" and contort our inner being into anxiety and doubt. But stress in itself is not destructive. In fact, we are always under stress in some form, even when we're asleep. It's when stress becomes distress that we're in trouble.

Distress occurs when we're not coping well with stress; it indicates that we're out of fellowship with God. In other words, distress results from reacting in our own power, instead of allowing the Holy Spirit to sit on the throne (to be in control) of our lives.

When God created us, He gave us bodies able to withstand stress, knowing we always would have to deal with it. But He intended for us to cope with stress by depending on Him. When we try to deal with it by ourselves, tension gets the best of us and stress becomes distress.

Properly handling stress begins with believing and trusting that God is in ultimate control of our lives. It requires relying on His Holy Spirit, whom He gives to all Christians, to empower us to live an abundant life. The abundant life is not a life devoid of stress; it is a full life of dependence on the Spirit for power to cope. In fact, God uses the stressful situations in our lives to teach us to live in His power instead of relying on our own resources, as we are prone to do. So we

85

actually can look on the stresses as positive, as Norma does, because they draw us closer to God.

In these next chapters, we'll look at some of the many causes of stress and how we can react without becoming distressed.

EXPECTATIONS

First, let's look at expectations. Much of stress comes from expectations: what we expect from ourselves and what we believe others expect from us . . . even what we think God expects from us. Often those expectations are that we must be perfect. Yet no one is perfect. Some of us go into parenthood expecting ourselves to be just that, however, and we expect the "joys of motherhood" to bury whatever frustrations might occur.

I had those expectations; I wanted to be the perfect mother. Before Darcy was born, I imagined myself always smiling and happy with my baby. I thought if I was cross or upset, I would destroy my child's self-image. When I did become angry or frustrated with Darcy, I was surprised that she continued to be a happy little girl. I finally realized that children's self-images are really not that brittle, and a little genuine love goes a long way. Of course, I found it hard to accept my anger toward Darcy, so I tried to stifle it, instead of dealing constructively with it.

What expectation of yourself haunts you the most? After reading the section on anger, you may now be expecting to *always* control your feelings of anger. Such a desire will pressure you tremendously and cause you to become discouraged if you slip back into your old pattern. That loss of confidence could cause you to give up hope of ever changing.

I encourage you to be realistic in your desire for victory. Realize you may fail, but that doesn't mean all is lost. Satan wants us to become discouraged and relive our failing. God wants us to confess, accept His forgiveness and *forgive ourselves*. Perfectionism (and pride) say, *I won't forgive myself.* Mercy says, *I forgive myself and will try again.* The fastest way to succeed is to forgive, start over and learn from our mistakes. Nineteenth century author James Lowell wrote, "Not failure but low aim is crime."[1]

Another unrealistic idea we have is thinking that only we are capable of caring for our children. At times others can and must care for our little ones. Whether it be our husbands, grandparents, babysitters or friends, they also can respond to our child's needs. They may not do everything exactly the way we do, but they still can give loving care.

We should allow others to care for them at times, because everyone needs time away from their children. Child abusers usually don't get many breaks away from their children. They are with them constantly. As a result, they have more difficulty gaining a positive perspective, which a little time alone can give.

Helen shared with me that she never left her two young daughters with anyone. Because of many problems, she was on the brink of child abuse. Her therapist told her to be separated from the girls for at least four hours each week. She obeyed him, but cried the whole time they were gone. Eventually she forced herself to find other things to occupy her mind, such as hobbies and a Bible study. Now she feels much better about herself and sees the benefits of having some time to herself. Her children also are happier because they have some playmates and are growing emotionally and intellectually at their preschool.

If it is difficult for you to find time alone, try setting up an exchange with a neighbor or friend. One week you care for her child one day and the next week, she takes yours for a day. Keep alternating and possibly add one or two friends. That would give you as many as three mornings a month free, at no expense.

The next expectation we want to talk about is what we think others demand of us. We may believe that other people will accept and love us only if we're perfect, or if we act the way they want us to behave.

If I can't allow others to see the true "me," which is anything but perfect, I still am struggling with poor self-image. If I don't want visitors unless my house is spotless, I'm focusing too much on other's expectations. If I can't go out of the house without my makeup on, I'm trying to people-please. If I'm afraid to reach out to someone who needs my friendship, for fear of being rejected, then other people are more important to me than God. If I hesitate to call someone to share that I'm angry with my kids, then I'm wearing a "mature Christian" mask.

My friend Beverly realized that she had become a people-pleaser. Other people's expectations were more important to her than her own opinions. She constantly experienced stress, because she couldn't meet everyone's expectations. Even when her words or actions pleased some of her friends, they displeased others.

She comments, "In time, I stopped and thought, *Who do I want to be? Do I want to be what others want me to be? Or, as a child of God, do I want to be what God wants?*

"I sat down and listed many situations that I'm often thrown into and subjects that I should have an opinion about. Then I wrote down by each what I believe and how I thought God wants me to react. On my list were topics like TV, books, jokes, prejudice . . . just about everything.

"Then, when I became involved in a conversation about a subject on my list, I knew who I was. I didn't have to be wishy-washy or a people-pleaser. I knew I was reacting as God wanted me to be, to the best of my ability.

"You know what else happened as a result of this? I felt a sense of greater self-worth. I knew what I stood for, and I experienced value as God's child."

As Beverly did, we can begin to be realistic and honest in our expectations—not trying to live according to what we think others expect of us. If they can't accept us as we truly are, then they aren't true friends. Our peace of mind and our relationship with God are more important than what other people think of us.

The final expectation is what we think God expects of us. Elaine believes the Lord expects more from her than she can possibly perform. As a result, she senses His condemnation. She says, "Our son was born prematurely and was not expected to survive. I know our prayers, as well as those by our family and friends, were swamping Jesus' ears. By God's grace and His alone, He allowed us to keep our son. All children are gifts from God, but we felt that our son was really special. I've often thought that the Lord must have something really special in mind for our little guy.

"But when I get angry with him—he's now two years old—I know the Lord is frowning. God watches every move I make, and I want so much for everything I do and say to please Him. I love the Lord and I know He can help me, but sometimes I feel so far away from Him."

Elaine is held by fear of a God who she thinks is strict and impersonal. She doesn't understand that even though He has called us to be holy even as He is holy (see 1 Peter 1:16), He also realizes we all are in a *process of growth*. Only Jesus is perfect. No one else has been or will ever be. God knows that. He is not surprised when it takes us a while to gain victory in an area of our lives. Satan wants us to feel ashamed and turn away from God, but God doesn't condemn us. He wants to forgive us and empower us to be successful next time. He longs to forgive and forget. How wonderful to think of God actually *forgetting* our sins!

Isaiah 1:18 assures us, "No matter how deep the stain of your sins, I can take it out and make you as clean as freshly fallen snow" (LB).

When we think of God's expectations, let's remember that He is patient with us and willing to forgive.

Yes, Elaine, God is watching your every move, but He is not frowning—He is smiling! He sees your love for Him. He sees your desire to please Him. He is satisfied because you are His child, not because you might act perfectly. He expects you to be growing and you are fulfilling that expectation.

WORRY

Arthur Somers Roche said, "Worry is a thin stream of fear trickling through the mind. If encouraged, it cuts a channel into which all other thoughts are drained."[2]

Worry is like that. It starts out as a trickle, a thought, an *I wonder,* and soon it's a raging river of fear and doubt. Many times that river ends its flow in a deep pool of anger.

Worry, like anger, is a word we sometimes try to cover up. We say, "I'm just concerned," or "I'm a little upset...but I'm not worried." Or we may think, *I may be fearful, but I'm not worried.* Heavens no!

Actually, concern, fear and worry are not the same. Concern is thinking about something, planning an action and putting it into effect.

90

Fear is based on external, real dangers and can protect us from harm.

Worry is a feeling of apprehension, tension or uneasiness about an approaching danger which does not stem from logic or a reasonable cause.[3]

Worry usually is occupied with the past or the future, but never with the present. So we worry in vain—it can't help the future or the past. It has been defined as a cycle of inefficient thought, whirling about a center of fear.

When we're caught up in that cycle, we fret about something and constantly think about it. We spend a great deal of time dwelling on a real or imagined problem. Worry can see only an unfortunate result in any situation, thus it prevents us from thinking clearly about our circumstances.

According to researcher Earl Nightingale, one study indicates that people worry about the following things in these percentages:

Things that never happen: 40%

Things of the past that can't be changed: 30%

Needless worries about health: 12%

Petty miscellaneous worries: 10%

Real, legitimate worries: 8%[4]

Since worry doesn't help us, let's look at six possible ways to eliminate that time and efficiency robber:

1. Think of why the thing we're worried about wouldn't be so bad after all.
2. Claim Romans 8:28.
3. Choose not to worry.
4. Think of solutions.
5. Accept what can't be changed.
6. Have godly priorities.

We will examine these solutions one at a time.

91

Healing the Angry Heart

1. THINK OF WHY THE THING WE'RE WORRIED ABOUT WOULDN'T BE SO BAD AFTER ALL

I began to have victory over worry after I heard seminar speaker Bill Gothard suggest this remedy. He said that when we are worried, we should think of the worst possible thing that could happen, and then think of reasons why it wouldn't be so bad after all. It works! Our worrying usually has no foundation in fact or truth, so by facing what we fear, we can conquer it. Then we can make a definite plan of action in case it does happen.

For example, putting my son, Mark, down for his nap is very important to me, because while he's asleep, I write and do my Bible study. Therefore, I easily can start to get upset and worry that he might not go to sleep. To combat my anxiety, I think of what I'll do if he doesn't go to sleep. I can invite a friend of his over to play and I still can study. Or I can do the errands I planned to do after he woke up, which might give me some time alone later while he and Darcy play. Or, since he'll be extra tired, I can put him to bed early and have more time to myself in the evening.

2. CLAIM ROMANS 8:28

Another way to take care of worry is to claim Romans 8:28: "And we know that all that happens to us is working for our good if we love God and are fitting into His plan" (LB). If God allows the situation we're worried about to happen, He will use it and we can praise Him for it. But let us not forget that this verse has a qualifier: all things work out for good *only* to those who love God and are submitting to His plans. To those people, God promises something good will always happen, even from an unpleasant situation.

Verna Birkey says, "God is the blessed controller of all things."[5] That statement often quiets my worries when I'm afraid that something unpleasant might happen. I remember that only those things that God allows will come into my life. His love filters out whatever is not for my best interest. That doesn't mean that unfortunate circumstances never will come my way, but that God will use whatever He permits, whether it be good or bad.

When I'm worried, I'm not trusting in God's loving filter. My worry often indicates I'm trying to take responsibility for something that God has not put me in charge of. Sometimes it belongs to my husband's area of responsibility, but I'm afraid he won't manage it well.

That has occurred when I see a stack of bills. Larry is in charge of paying them, according to our mutual agreement, but I start to feel nervous when I see them pile up. He's often paid late charges when he's been too busy to get to them, but as a result, he's getting more prompt. And I'm learning to trust God more to move in my husband's life.

3. CHOOSE NOT TO WORRY

Just as we can change negative self-talk into good self-image, so can we choose not to worry. The same principles in 2 Corinthians 10:5 apply to both: "taking every thought captive to the obedience of Christ."

Remember the darts of negative self-talk, which we can choose to accept or reject? We have the same choice with the darts of worried thoughts. Philippians 4:6,7 exhorts us, "Be anxious (worried) for nothing, but in everything by prayer and supplication with thanksgiving let your requests be made known to God. And the peace of God, which surpasses all comprehension, shall guard your hearts and your minds in Christ Jesus."

As we pray and trust God to help us, His peace will strengthen us to reject worried thoughts.

Judy is learning victory over worry. Every time she identifies worried thoughts, she prays for God's help and then consciously chooses to think of an incident when God turned one of her worries into a blessing. Then her worries recede.

4. THINK OF SOLUTIONS

Instead of focusing on our worries, we need to think of solutions. We should list all our worries and anxieties, and then write a list of possible solutions. Usually just pinpointing them, especially on paper, will help us see that they aren't as bad as we imagined. Then we can begin to work actively on solutions.

I've listed my worries and then sat there thinking, "Now, there must be more things I can write down. This isn't very much to feel stressed about."

Yet, those few things had boggled my mind into inefficiency and anxiety. Like a sponge in water, they had swelled to fill my mind until I couldn't think straight, and I was reacting in anger.

Once I looked my worries square in the eye, they became solvable.

5. ACCEPT WHAT CAN'T BE CHANGED

Worry concentrates on those things we can't change and makes us feel like we should do something about them. Worry says we'll be happy if we change our spouses. Anxiety suggests we're going to go bankrupt if the breadwinner doesn't get that raise. Worry tells us our friends won't accept us unless we move into a larger home. It goes on and on.

Many things in life are beyond our power. But Someone can change things, so we must leave them to Jesus. Reinhold Niebuhr's prayer can help us in this area, "God, give us grace to accept with serenity the things that cannot be changed, courage to change the things that should be changed, and the

94

wisdom to distinguish one from the other." Trusting in God in this area will eliminate some stress in our lives.

6. HAVE GODLY PRIORITIES

In Matthew 6:28-34, Jesus told us not to worry about the material and worldly things of our lives. He reminded us that God takes care of even the birds and flowers, and we're more important to Him than they are. What is really important, what we should be concerned about, are the true values of life: seeking first the kingdom of God and His righteousness. Once we do that, He promises to supply all our other needs. One of our problems, though, is that we don't always agree with God about what our true needs are. We must acquire God's viewpoint.

Along with having godly priorities, we need to weed out what is unimportant in dealing with our children. When I start getting uptight about Darcy not putting in hair barrettes, or wanting to wear clashing colors out to play, or preferring oranges to apples, then I am building unimportant issues into a cold war. You may laugh at my examples, but I actually have become angry over those very things. They sound silly now, but at the moment, they seemed so vital.

I can tell I'm taking life too seriously when those kinds of issues pressure me. I'm learning to allow Darcy to make decisions, so she can be her own person and feel good about herself. That may mean I watch her go out to play with hair in her eyes and wearing a green blouse and purple skirt!

Verse 34 tells us to have the right priority of living one day at a time. It says, "Therefore do not be anxious for tomorrow; for tomorrow will care for itself. Each day has enough trouble of its own." That doesn't mean we don't set goals. It means we emphasize the present and enjoy each day to the fullest, without worrying about what is around the corner.

Healing the Angry Heart

God wants us to enjoy an abundant life. We rob ourselves of that joy by dwelling on the past, which can't be changed, and on the future, which we can depend upon God to take care of.

WHAT YOU CAN DO

1. If you do not have any time away from your children, find a way to make some time for yourself.
2. Memorize Philippians 1:6.
3. Examine the solutions for worry and determine which you will use.

Chapter 10

Over-Commitments and Time Pressures

"Oh, no. I'm going to be late. I shouldn't have stayed so long visiting Judy at the hospital."

My mind was clouded with all the things I still had to do before making my way to the dentist. My foot pushed down the accelerator and worry excused the speed. I still had to pick up Mark from home and Darcy from school. *Oh, why did they ask me to be fifteen minutes early for the appointment?*

I pulled into the driveway and rushed into the house. Larry lay on the couch, while Mark sat on the floor with his shoes and shirt off. I hit the ceiling. "Why isn't Mark ready? You know I have to be at the dentist in a few minutes. Why don't you have him dressed?" My yelling filled the rooms as I rushed throughout the house, collecting Mark's shoes and shirt. Larry looked at me in disbelief, but I didn't care. I felt tense and angry.

Next we rushed to Darcy's school to pick her up. Then we were on our way. The twenty-minute drive to the office would put us ten minutes late, but I hoped to shave off a few minutes by speeding. I soon realized, though, that God was trying to get my attention, as I hit every red signal and waited, trapped behind slow trucks. "Father, I have to get going. I'm late! Please hurry things along."

He seemed to be saying, "Slow down and trust me." But I didn't want to listen. I told them I would be there early; now they would think I'm undependable. My frustration and tension clouded whatever faith or common sense I possessed.

When I pushed open the dentist's office door, with Mark crying and Darcy fearful of my tension, the receptionist did not even notice that we were late. In fact, we had to wait several minutes before being called in. Suddenly, all my hurrying seemed so stupid and senseless. I slumped into a chair, weak and perspiring. Frustration had again overwhelmed me.

When pressures become too great because we have too much to do and not enough time, we easily translate our tension into anger at our children. If we are too busy, then we haven't followed the priorites God wants for us. As a result, over-commitment and time pressures can cause frustration and anger to rule our lives.

Let's talk about these issues and how we can handle the stress from them.

OVER-COMMITMENT

General Eisenhower is quoted as saying, "The urgent is seldom important, and the important is seldom urgent." In today's society, we are victimized by the urgent. Urgent demands cause us to become over-committed at the expense of our families. *They* don't seem urgent, because they are always around. We have the impression that we have our whole future in which to build our relationships with them. So the dishes, housecleaning, earning a living, shopping or a friend's problems tend to catch and hold our attention more easily than our husband or children. But our family is important. We need to ensure that the urgent doesn't crowd them out of our priorities.

If we take an honest look at the value of urgent demands, we find that they aren't as important as we thought. We may feel pressured to fulfill some activity, yet, we easily could do without it. Eliminating it would lessen the stress we're under, and the important things of life would receive our attention.

Have you noticed that the things we must do over and over again often pressure us the most, even though the tasks are never completely finished? The daily duties of housework, which we will repeat, take time away from our children. But that special time with our child will be lost forever. We must focus on what is the most valuable.

A good way to determine the importance of something is to ask, "Will it influence the future? Will it be significant a year, five years or even ten years from now? The only areas that retain their value over time are relationships. People are the only "things" that will be in heaven with us.

When I become over-committed, I usually have not said no often enough. Because of my past insecurity and poor self-image, I have a hard time refusing responsibilities. I don't want to disappoint people or assert myself.

I *am* seeing progress, though. By establishing goals and priorites, I am better equipped to decide what God really wants me to do. I also found greater strength to say no after I heard that, "A need is not necessarily a call." This adage helps me remember that, just because someone says "help," doesn't mean I'm necessarily the one who's supposed to jump. I need to be sure that God is calling me, rather than simply responding to everyone who thinks I'm supposed to do something.

Most of us who can't say no worry that if we don't do it, it won't get done. This is especially fear-provoking when we see a worthy cause lacking help. But if we take on a job to which God has not called us, we are depriving someone else of the responsibility—and the blessing He wanted them to have. Maybe that other person is trying to get up enough courage to step out in faith. Or maybe they are waiting to see if someone else accepts it. They believe that if no one does, then God is confirming that they should take the job.

If each one of us seeks where God wants us to be—what area of service or work He desires for us—we will be able to determine our priorities more easily and we will not feel so pressured to do more than He wants us to do.

As we clarify our priorities, we can ask ourselves, "What will happen if this activity is not done at all?" If we answer "nothing," that is our clue to give it low priority. Worry can make us assume that something awful will happen if it isn't done, but when we think clearly about it, we may realize that the consequences would be minimal.

Recently every leader in a woman's program at our church resigned. At the reorganization meeting, no one seemed thrilled about the prospect of taking over. I sat there almost ready to volunteer, because I didn't want to see the excellent program cancelled. I had to keep telling myself, "God is not calling me to this responsibility," yet I didn't know what He had for me. It took all my strength to resist the impulse to jump in.

I heard the other day that a whole new group of women are heading the program, most of whom weren't even at the meeting. They have some exciting new ideas.

In the meantime, I was challenged to teach a new class at church that is exactly in line with my goals and desires. I'm so glad I didn't volunteer to be where God didn't want me! Obeying Him kept me from being over-committed, and I could accept what He really desired for me.

TIME PRESSURES

Just as being over-committed applies stress to us, so do time pressures. We all could use an extra hour or two each day, right? Oh . . . three? Do I hear four? I thought so.

Time pressure happens when we try to get too much done, and then the phone rings with an unexpected plea for help, or a child is sick, or . . . etc. The possibilities are endless.

The pressures of demands on our time can result from poor planning or unexpected circumstances. Either way, we run out of time before we run out of things to do.

Suzanne knows about running out of time. She overslept, the oatmeal boiled over as she changed the baby, she's late for a meeting, and as she tries to race out the door, the baby spits up on her white dress.

At times like that, there's not much that Suzanne, or any of us, can do. Instead of getting angry (which won't cause the clock's hands to go backwards), we might as well relax and take it in stride. Sure, Suzanne shouldn't have overslept, and she should have watched the oatmeal closer, but what can she do when the baby spits up? She can't change the past. She only can choose how she will react at that moment. Whether she decides to get angry or relax and trust the Lord probably will determine how the rest of her day goes.

Charles Swindoll says, "Humans are strange creatures. We run faster when we lose our way. Instead of pausing to regroup, we ricochet from place to place."[1]

Healing the Angry Heart

Sometimes, in situations similar to Suzanne's, I ricochet from place to place. I keep running faster and faster, hoping time will slow down. All that happens are more disasters and anger.

At other times, I stop, pray, relax and trust the Lord. What a difference that makes in my attitude and the rest of the day. I also am learning to plan ahead as well as I can. Then, if unexpected situations arise, I flow with what the Lord has decided.

My peace in these events hinges upon whether I've dedicated my day to the Lord in the morning. . . and meant it. Once I have, I can rest and relax, knowing that God is in control of my day, so I don't need to be. Often I pray that no phone calls will come except those to which He wants me to respond. I ask for wisdom to know what future plans to make. Sometimes I need to ask for strength to admit when I've taken on too much. Then I must bow out or ask for someone's help.

Time pressures are another area in which I must accept my limitations and realize I can't do everything. I also need to ask, "If I'm late, does it really matter that much? If something doesn't get done, will the world fall apart?" No matter what happens, I need to make sure I don't fall apart with an angry attitude.

I consider myself a dependable person and, as a result, my commitments are almost life-death responsibilities for me. I even get upset if I have to cancel a babysitter. But I'm trying to learn to relax and let stress "roll off my back."

Two principles have helped me tremendously in trusting God for time pressures. The first is: *God is in control.* When I start to feel frazzled and rushed, I can take several deep breaths and remember that God's power is so strong that He is controlling everything in my life. I simply need to trust

Him, and He'll work things out.

I had to apply that principle one morning as I worked on a project that was due for a meeting that evening. A friend called to say she had a counseling appointment with her pastor that afternoon, and she wanted me to go with her for support. I was thrilled she had scheduled it, since I'd been trying to get her into counseling for a long time. I knew the project needed to be done, but the Lord seemed to prompt me to say I'd go with her. So I did.

After returning home, the phone rang. It was the woman in charge of the meeting, saying it had been cancelled.

Not all my stressful circumstances work out that smoothly, but the more I trust God for every area of His control, the more stress isn't becoming distress in my life.

The second principle that I've found helpful is: *God will give me enough time to do what He wants me to do.* If God wants me to accomplish something, I just need to obey Him minute by minute, based on the priorities He has given me, and He will provide the time to finish it. I also remember that God is more concerned with my attitude than with whether or not I complete a project. Therefore, my reactions are even more important than my performance.

This past summer I was given a deadline of October 1 to complete the revision of this book. The children were home and it was very difficult to work on it. I tried to squeeze in as much time as possible, but I kept getting sidetracked by their interruptions and needs. At times, I started to feel tense and angry. I wanted to shout, "Just leave me alone. I've got to work on this."

Then I remembered my priorities: God, husband, children . . . writing. I told myself that my family was more important than this book and that God would give me enough time to do this if He wanted me to do it.

Now it's September. The kids are in school and my days are free to write. I'm a little behind, but (say it with me!) "God will give me enough time to do what He wants me to do." Therefore, I'm obeying Him by using my time efficiently, and I'm sure that I will complete it by His deadline.

SETTING PRIORITIES

Setting priorities can prevent us from being over-committed and can help us cope with time pressures.

When we have many things to do, we can list them and prioritize them according to this method:

#1: Must do
#2: Should do
#3: Can do

Then we can take all the "#1s" and break them down into 1s, 2s and 3s. By doing all the #1s first, we establish direction for our lives.

This technique released me from stress just the other day. So many things were racing through my head that I was almost in tears, worrying about what I needed to do. I couldn't think clearly enough to decide where to start first. I sat down and listed all the things that clamored to be done, and I was amazed to find there weren't as many as I thought. It just seemed like it because I felt so confused and helpless, and out of control. But seeing them written down, and then prioritized by #1s, #2s, and #3s, enabled me to see where to start. I had a plan to follow. My confusion disappeared and I got everything done.

If you are a mother of small children, you may seem never to accomplish anything, yet you are too busy to do the many things you'd like to do. I constantly felt that way when Darcy and Mark were very young (and I still do sometimes). But when I actually wrote down, minute by minute, what I did all day, I discovered that I wasn't wasting time. Young children simply require a great deal of time and attention. That made me feel better. I was more content, knowing it wouldn't always be that way. Now that they are older, I'm enjoying some freedom and doing many of the projects I'd always wanted to do.

Remember Suzanne, who we mentioned earlier? She's standing at the door in her burped-on white dress, knowing she has two choices, anger or trust. She takes a deep breath and starts to laugh, as tears roll down her cheeks.

Now her mascara is running, so after she puts the baby down she fixes her makeup and changes her clothes. Heading for the door a second time, she figures she'll be about twenty minutes late for the meeting.

When she arrives, no one is there. Ten minutes later, when her friends walk in the door, she asks what time the meeting was supposed to start.

"Nine-thirty. What time did you think?" they question.

"Nine o'clock," she says, grinning.

WHAT YOU CAN DO

1. Identify the priorities in your life.
2. Next time you feel pressured, prioritize your list.

Chapter 11

Reactions to Stress

The Chinese use two picture-words for *crisis*. The same characters also are used to communicate *danger* and *opportunity*. The Chinese apparently recognize that the crises—the stresses—in a mother's life actually are opportunities to realize fully the potential of her personality.

James 1:2-4 says the same thing, with a little paraphrasing from my own interpretation: "Dear sisters, is your life full of stress and pressure? Then be happy, for when the way is rough, your patience has a chance to grow. So let it grow, and don't get angry instead. For when your patience is finally in full bloom, then you will be ready for any kind of crisis; you'll be strong in character, full and complete" (my paraphrase of *The Living Bible*).

So let's look at stress as positive—as a wonderful

opportunity to grow into maturity and be molded into the image of Christ! If we see stress as an occasion for growth, instead of as a cursed evil, we can look it square in the eye and not get angry and frustrated.

Let's examine five constructive reactions to stress, from which we can choose when tension makes us want to scream. These choices are based on the acrostic REACT:

R: readjust
E: express
A: attack
C: compromise
T: turn

READJUST

In handling stress, we may need to readjust our goals or expectations. Perhaps we're expecting too much from ourselves or others, or maybe the goal we've set is too difficult or unattainable. Possibly we've realized that our goal is not God's will, so we need to seek Him for a new plan.

Sometimes we are too close to a situation to see it realistically, so we should consult someone else, preferably a professional counselor. A person outside our circumstances can see our problem more clearly and offer advice. Then we can adjust our attitude accordingly.

EXPRESS

Just as we must express our anger in order to deal with it, so must we express our stress. Verbalizing stress can release some pressure and make other people aware of our situation. We might say, "I'm under a lot of stress right now, so I don't think I can handle that." "Please pray for me; I'm really feeling pressured right now because of _____." Or, "I'm deep in thought about something that's bothering me. We can play that game in fifteen minutes, O.K.?"

Our children and mates would prefer that we tell them when we're under strain, rather than letting it surface in anger, coldness or harsh words.

Another positive way to express our stress is to write about it. Keeping a diary or journal has been a wonderful outlet for me. I've found that writing down my thoughts and feelings is good therapy. It also encourages me to read past entries about how upsetting situations worked out. Usually, their importance diminished with time. This reminds me that my present unnerving circumstance also will work out, with God's help.

ATTACK

When we fully realize the pressure and decide how to deal with it appropriately, we can attack the problem head-on. Maybe we need to talk it over with our spouse or a friend, or talk into a tape recorder and then play it back to listen for what we're really concerned about. We also can prioritize the demands on us, or delegate some of our responsibilities to others when we have too many things to do.

We need to get the stress out in the open and deal with it, rather than leaving it cooped up inside of us, where it can turn into worry or anger. We can examine it by asking, "What is God trying to teach me through this pressure?" or "What quality is He building in my life by allowing this stress?" Our Lord is very efficient and He uses every circumstance in our lives to draw us closer to Him. As we seek His wisdom, He will guide us in how to handle each pressure so that it benefits us and glorifies Him.

COMPROMISE

We can give and take in a situation, knowing it will help us deal with the stress. We may not get everything we want, but at least we will relieve the pressure before we lash out at someone.

Healing the Angry Heart

I remember one time when I felt distressed and couldn't see the light at the end of the tunnel. I talked the problem over with a friend, and she suggested a very satisfactory compromise. I was a little embarrassed that I hadn't thought of it myself, but I had been so determined to get my way that I couldn't see any other viewpoint.

Compromise doesn't mean giving in on moral issues that the Bible specifically addresses. God's word always should be our authority, but we also should listen to and tolerate other's suggestions and ideas, and take into account their thoughts. God often uses others to show us how to change.

TURN

Turning back or withdrawing can be acceptable if we've taken on too much and must give something up. We may need to go away for a weekend to get a different perspective, or resign from a position that has too much pressure. Turning back is not defeat; it is realizing our limitations and abilities, and adapting accordingly.

When you are under stress, think of yourself as a building that God is making. When a contractor builds a house, he has in mind how beautiful his home will turn out to be. The blueprints and work orders call for the materials and labor necessary to accomplish his plan.

God's plan for our lives is that we each gain a unique personality that radiates the image of His wonderful Son, Jesus. As He labors to build that into us, one tool He uses is stress.

But sometimes we argue with God. "Lord, you didn't drill that many holes in Fred. And you gave Alice more bedrooms. Ouch! Why do you have to pour cement for the foundation? It's so heavy. And Lord, I just can't handle two stories. By the way, I want to have french doors into the dining room. What? No dining room? And why do they have to put tile on my roof?

Oh, I can't stand all this pounding. Father, you don't know what you're doing."

The Lord replies, "My child, I *do* know what I'm doing. Without the work that I'm doing on you now, you would leak and the wind would blow right through you. Just trust Me. You're going to be a beautiful home that is a haven for your family. You'll be a strong fortress for others to come into from the cold and darkness. 'I know the plans I have for you . . . plans for welfare and not for evil, to give you a future and a hope'" (Jeremiah 29:11, RSV).

As we learn to trust God more, we will find it easier to relax, knowing that He will not give us more stress than we can handle in His power, and that He will use the stress He allows to conform us to Christ's image.

WHAT YOU CAN DO
1. Memorize the REACT choices for responding to stress and choose one or more of them when you experience stress.
2. Memorize one or more of these scriptures:
   Proverbs 3:5,6
   Isaiah 26:3
   Isaiah 41:10,13
   1 Peter 5:7
   Psalm 32:8
   Psalm 42:5

111

Chapter 12
Hope for Depression

Sometimes, in the midst of difficult circumstances, when stress seems to overwhelm us, we experience depression. The stress might not cause the depression, but it may be one of many contributing factors.

Julianne was depressed. She had no hope. She slept most of the time, didn't have the energy to clean her house and rejected her friends' offers to take her out.

When I talked to her about the Lord, she often asked, "Has God rejected me? I'm so afraid I've done something wrong and He won't forgive me."

I assured her of His constant love, but it didn't seem to register. Her depressed mind couldn't absorb truth.

Depressed people, like Julianne, have no hope that things will get better, no hope that someone can help, no hope that anyone loves them or cares. They give up.

A depressed housewife may leave the housework undone, not go anywhere, stay in one room the whole day, not get dressed, and begin to depend upon alcohol or drugs. A depressed man may lose all ambition in his job, neglect his hobbies, and spend his evenings and weekends watching television, surrounded by empty beer cans. Yet, even though they lack energy, their depression can flare up into anger. So it is important to deal with depression and eliminate it at its source.

CAUSES OF DEPRESSION

The following list of factors which may lead to depression is by no means inclusive, and people certainly can experience these without suffering depression. Yet, we will examine each of these five potential causes and discuss how to keep them from leading to depression, and possibly anger:

1. Discouragement
2. Self-pity
3. Success
4. Exhaustion
5. Physical reactions

1. DISCOURAGEMENT

Depression usually starts with discouragement. When discouragement first hits us, we tend to decrease our involvement with people and activities. When we need people the most, we separate ourselves from the relationships that can strengthen us. Our pride prevents us from saying, "Help! I'm discouraged." We don't want to be vulnerable. We don't want to let people see that our Christian mask is on a little crooked. Someone may sincerely ask me, "How are you?" and I'll reply, "Oh, just fantastic," even though I'm hurting so bad that I've cried all day.

As soon as we back away, we become more discouraged. Then depression can take over. If this cycle continues, we shut ourselves off from everyone and everything, thus becoming totally entrenched in our depression. That is why we shouldn't withdraw when discouragement first hits us. If we are over-committed, we may need to cut back, but we should maintain our daily routine and communicate with others.

Psalm 42:5 offers us practical guidelines for discouragement: "Why are you in despair, O my soul? And why have you become disturbed within me? Hope in God, for I shall again praise Him for the help of His presence."

This verse encourages us to hope in God and turn our thoughts to praising Him. Focusing on God and the "help of His presence," instead of on our troubles and our responsibilities, can renew our optimism.

Not long ago, I was discouraged as I focused on my stressful circumstances. I lost hope of God's goodness and ability to rescue me. It was a Sunday afternoon, and I moped around the house feeling sorry for myself. I finally went to bed, thinking that a nap might help me, but it didn't.

Then the phone rang. It was Carolyn, a friend I hadn't spoken with for a while. She said God kept putting me on her mind that afternoon, and she wondered if we could go to the evening church service together. I acted as if I felt fine, and agreed to go with her. Then, on the way to church, I told her about my bad day, and I ended up crying throughout the service as our pastor spoke on depression. I told her later, "I never could have sat through that sermon, even though I needed to hear it, without your quiet acceptance beside me."

Carolyn was the support God provided to get me through my crisis. As a result, I again could focus on God's love for me and restore my trust that God would take care of the situation, which He did.

2. *SELF-PITY*

At the very core of depression is the beast of self-pity. We might complain: "Nothing goes my way. No one understands. No one loves me." When I'm depressed, Larry reminds me I'm having a pity party. I don't like to hear that—because it's true! Depression focuses only on me. I become the most important person in the world; life has dealt me an unfair blow. I don't like it.

When I'm bogged down in self-pity, remembering the blessing and benefits I enjoy can be powerful therapy. Depression breeds and thrives on negative thinking, so we need to correct each negative thought.

H. Norman Wright suggests that we tell ourselves, "O.K., I am depressed. There are reasons why I'm depressed and they are valid reasons. My depression is telling me that something is bothering me about the way I am living my life. While it is very painful, it may help me to understand myself better. I'm going to learn something from this experience. And I *am* going to feel better."[1] We should say this to ourselves as many times a day as needed.

Sometimes just thinking positively is not enough, though. We may need to seek the help of a friend or a professional counselor. We see the situation from our limited perspective, but as we express our thoughts and feelings to someone else, that person can see the total picture and help us be objective.

We need objective thinking because self-pity can make us oversensitive to others' words and actions. We can misinterpret when we process everything through the gauze of feeling sorry for ourselves. We may suspiciously perceive a friend's comment as an insult, or our mate's questioning look as condemnation. If we do, we need to respond with trust, acknowledging their love and concern for us.

3. SUCCESS

Though it may sound unusual, success can cause depression. Have you ever noticed how vulnerable you are after a time of great victory or celebration? Even the joy of special holidays, like Christmas, can crash down into depression after the festivities end. The sameness, the daily duties of life, set in and life no longer is exciting. It is boring!

I remember feeling discouraged after successfully ministering to some people. The next week, I said something foolish to a group of friends. I was so upset about what they thought of me that I became depressed—all the joy of the previous week's victory evaporated. I could think only about me and my image to others.

Be especially careful after victorious times. You may even be experiencing a new control over your anger, and you are praising the Lord. That's great. But if you experience a set back, don't let that discourage you. Just ask God's forgiveness and continue on. Be wary, realizing that sampling victory doesn't mean you can stop depending on God.

4. EXHAUSTION

Exhaustion is another possible cause of depression. As mothers, we can be so busy that we don't take care of our own needs. Caring for children often makes it difficult for us to eat healthfully and get enough sleep or exercise. Unfortunately, our children end up paying in the end if we become depressed or angry.

During the period of time when anger controlled me, I was awake several times a night nursing Mark. More tired than I realized, I easily flew off the handle, because my patience level was low. As soon as I started taking naps, I saw a measurable improvement in my ability to cope.

5. *PHYSICAL REACTIONS*

Finally, other physical causes can create depression, such as chemical imbalances in our bodies, pre-menstrual syndrome (PMS), excessive sugar intake and certain diseases.

Eating too much sugar is a fast way for me to become depressed and easily angered. I'm growing in my ability to resist sweets, because I know if I eat them, I'll be low on patience the next day.

My friend Teri discovered that she has PMS. Since she began taking medication, she's noticed a tremendous difference in her tolerance level toward her young children. Now she wonders how she ever survived during that time when she reacted so angrily.

SOLUTIONS FOR DEPRESSION

Whenever depression begins to hit us, we can fight back and regain a positive outlook. This chart summarizes some ways to combat depression at its source.

CAUSE	SOLUTION
1. Discouragement	Choosing to complete the work God has given us to do, involvement, activity.
2. Self-pity	Focusing on our blessings, thinking positively, objective viewpoint.
3. Success	Continued dependence on God, keeping our eyes off our own accomplishments and giving God the credit.
4. Exhaustion	Rest, meeting our physical needs, exercise.

| 5. Physical (chemical im- balance, PMS, excessive sugar intake, disease) | Counseling, medication, eating healthfully, physical examination. |

We also can defeat depression by becoming involved in a new purpose and reason for living—a new mission. As a result, we will be filled with new enthusiasm for life. We'll feel important and useful.

God has a purpose for each of our lives. Maybe His mission for you is to reach out to others who have similar problems. Or perhaps you could help the disadvantaged or the handicapped. Another possibility is to make a new friend or reestablish a relationship. Even writing one uplifting letter each week to someone who needs encouragement can give us purpose.

By reaching out, helping others, and thus serving God, we won't have time to brood about our problems or focus too much on ourselves. We'll have others to think about, which can help prevent discouragement, self-pity, success, exhaustion or physical problems from turning into depression.

Remember Julianne? She called me the other day. After being in a deep depression for almost a year, she's praising the Lord. She became involved in Bible studies and went to an inner healing class. Over a few weeks' time, she began to see a difference in her attitudes. Now she's healed! She was cleaning her house when she called. Her voice was strong, clear and decisive. She said she knows that the Lord has not deserted her, and that He loves and accepts her. That was wonderful to hear!

WHAT YOU CAN DO

1. If you are depressed, determine the probable cause and follow the corresponding solution.

Healing the Angry Heart

2. Memorize Psalm 42:5: "Why am I so sad? Why am I so troubled? I will put my hope in God, and once again I will praise Him, my Savior and my God" (GNB).

Section IV

Discipline Your Child Effectively

Chapter 13
Some Valuable Differences

"Please don't do that."

"You're doing it again!"

"I've told you before not to do that!"

"How many times do I have to tell you—*Don't do that!*"

I often went through that downward spiral of anger and exasperation. It usually ended in an angry outburst at Darcy. I wanted her to be an obedient, disciplined child, yet I soon realized that first I needed to be disciplined. That wasn't easy! As a result, disciplining Darcy became an inconsistent, angry merry-go-round.

Many Christians believe that disciplining children means spanking them for every misdeed. But effective discipline involves training our children and controlling ourselves while we do it. That's why this section follows our examination of self-image, anger and stress. Once we begin to have victory in those areas, we can control ourselves as we guide our children.

Darcy took her first steps as a toddler before I took that initial step of self-discipline. I tried to control her with angry looks and harsh words. I thought that being upset with her would cause her to behave properly. I reasoned, *She won't want me to be angry with her, therefore, she'll do what I want her to do.* When she continued to disobey, I concluded, I *guess I'll have to become even more angry so she won't do that again!*

But, of course, it didn't work, because anger doesn't motivate anyone to obey! It may make them fearful, and they may act correctly for a short while, but in the long run, *anger does not instill obedience!*

I can see now that if I had disciplined Darcy correctly, I could have alleviated most of the anger and abuse I heaped upon her.

THREE LEVELS OF DISCIPLINE

The foundation for disciplining correctly is an understanding of what discipline really is. Rather than being simply punishment, actually, discipline has three levels:

1. Instruction: giving guidelines and verbally telling the child how to do something correctly.
2. Training: guiding him, working with him, being alongside as he learns.
3. Correction: appropriate measures taken when he disobeys, after he understands and can perform.

We have a beautiful example in Jesus as He taught and discipled His followers. He spent much time and effort instructing, training and correcting them. They became His disciples—disciplined ones. Then, when He was gone, they could follow His teachings through the empowering of the Holy Spirit.

Will our children continue to obey our teachings even when we aren't with them? They probably will if we have instructed, trained and corrected them adequately. In a sense, they become our disciples.

DIFFERENCE BETWEEN PUNISHMENT AND DISCIPLINE

In learning about the three levels of discipline, I began to understand the difference between discipline and punishment, and that discovery helped me stay in control.

Punishment implies hurting someone in retribution or paying them back for an offense. We punish to satisfy anger or the requirements of our society's legal system. It is done for our sake, not for the sake of the wrongdoer.

Discipline, on the other hand, is for the sake of the child; to help him improve himself or to learn a lesson that will make him a better person. It's the idea of developing within our child self-control and respect for authority.

Dr. Bruce Narramore gives us a clear explanation of this difference in a chart from his book, *Help! I'm a Parent!*[1]

	PUNISHMENT	DISCIPLINE
Purpose	To inflict penalty for an offense	To train for correction and maturity
Focus	Past misdeeds	Future correct acts
Attitude	Hostility and frustration on the part of the parent	Love and concern on the part of the parent
Resulting emotion in the child	Fear and guilt	Security

125

Healing the Angry Heart

Once I realized this distinction, I knew I had been punishing Darcy instead of disciplining her. I was trying to pay her back for her misdeeds, which I took personally, instead of wanting to train her for the future.

When I changed my purpose from punishing to training, I found I more often could discipline her without losing control. Before, it seemed that my anger had to be part of the punishment to emphasize the "badness" of her past actions. I would say something like, "I am spanking you because you did something wrong."

When I changed my focus, I began to want her to remember to obey next time. Therefore, as I spoke to her during the disciplining process, I would say, "I am disciplining you so that you will remember not to do that again." The correction became geared to the future instead of to the past. That gave me hope, because I knew it would make her obedient, in the long run.

DISCIPLINING IS A PROCESS

In the long run! As I spanked Darcy, I often thought, *If only I could spank you long enough and hard enough, then you'd be perfect I and you wouldn't give me any more problems!*

My perfectionist expectations were surfacing again. I wanted Darcy to be perfect, even though I couldn't be. I wanted to believe that correcting her one time would permanently affect her. Then I became frustrated when she did the same thing over and over again.

Somehow God finally made me realize that disciplining is a long-range process. It takes effort and concentration over a long period. In fact, my correcting Darcy would cause her to try it again, to test me to see if I would be consistent and if I really meant what I had said. This is why we shouldn't give up, thinking, "See? Disciplining doesn't work!" If we persevere, we will see results eventually.

CONSISTENCY

When we consistently show them the results of their actions, we will see our children's behavior improve. Yet it is difficult to be consistent.

Consistency is defined as "conformity with previous practice; agreement with what has already been done." The opposite is disciplining for a misbehavior on some occasions and ignoring the same wrongdoing other times.

Consistency also is defined as "the predictability of a parent's behavior." It is important because it satisfies the child's need for safety; he knows how his parent will act and he feels safe and secure. When we're inconsistent, he continues to misbehave to try to make us correct him and cause him to feel secure.

Most of us want to be consistent—why is it so difficult? For one thing, we're either lazy, too busy, or too engrossed in what we're doing to set it aside to correct a misbehaving child. It's difficult to inconvenience ourselves temporarily. But if we will decide to do it, in obedience to God's command, life will be more peaceful. It will result in our child learning to behave properly and to obey.

Another stumbling block to consistency is that we avoid confronting the child because we anticipate conflict. This was my underlying reason for rationalizing, *I've only given Darcy one warning about that today, so I'll let it slide this time.* Or, *Well, she didn't really do anything bad enough to deserve a spanking.* But that kind of thinking only created more battles.

We also may rationalize that we need to be patient. Did you know it is possible to be *too patient?* We can be so longsuffering that we put off correction, thinking our patience will give our children time to learn. In reality, only our involvement will cause them to make the right choices.

In the meantime, all their small incidents of disobedience can build up anger within us, and eventually we could explode. Therefore, we should use our patience to discipline *calmly* and *immediately,* not to keep waiting for obedience, which will never come on its own.

We need to give the same consequence every time, directly after the child disobeys. It doesn't matter how long ago we gave the rule, or even how often they already have obeyed it. Each and every time they break the rule or disobey the command, they must receive the same, fair correction. Then we will see results, and our love will not turn into anger.

Joyce realized the value of consistent disciplining as she saw her son become more obedient. She says, "Jason now knows that when I count 'one . . . two . . . ,' he'd better stop what he's doing wrong or start doing what he's supposed to. If I reach three, I'm committed to move my body calmly, but with determination, in his direction. Sometimes, it's difficult to drop what I'm doing, but I already am seeing the result in Jason's improved behavior."

THE BENEFITS OF DISCIPLINING

As our children learn to obey, they will realize that being disciplined has many benefits. We also need to recognize those advantages, so that we'll be motivated to train our children.

The most important benefit is that our children will learn self-control and respect for authority. With those attitudes, we can expect well-mannered, pleasant children who will not grieve us in later years.

Another aspect that we sometimes forget is that discipline shows our child that we love him. The child who is trained believes he's important; that he belongs to the family. He knows we love him, because we take the time and effort to teach him.

God commands us to discipline our children, and He promises benefits. "Teach a child to choose the right path, and when he is older he will remain upon it" (Proverbs 22:6, LB). "Discipline your son and he will give you happiness and peace of mind" (Proverbs 29:17, LB). Hebrews 12:5-11 gives many other benefits: an abundant life (verse 9), holiness (verse 10), peaceful fruit of righteousness (verse 11).

WILLFUL DISOBEDIENCE VS.
CHILDISH IRRESPONSIBILITY

One important thing that we should know about is what Dr. James Dobson often calls the difference between willful disobedience and childish irresponsibility. Willful disobedience is when the child intentionally disobeys, knowing he's doing something wrong. Childish irresponsibility is when the child does something wrong, but it is because of his immaturity. It is a mistake or an accident.

Quite often children do the wrong thing because they are children! They are in the process of learning and are not yet consistent in their behavior. The difference between defiant behavior and immaturity lies in the child's intention. For example, throwing food would be willful, whereas spilling a glass of milk most likely is irresponsibility. Did he intend to do wrong or was it an accident?

Either way, we may still need to discipline him to teach him responsibility, but the consequences will be different in each case. When he spills the milk, he should wipe it up himself. For throwing food, he could be sent to his room for a few minutes, or we might take away his meal.

No matter what the situation, it is important to stay calm and discipline him consistently. We also should remember, he'll naturally outgrow childish irresponsibility; we have to help him overcome willful disobedience.

POWER STRUGGLE

When a child acts in willful disobedience, the conflict with the parent may turn into a "power struggle," unless the parent prevents it. H. Norman Wright defines a power struggle as a child challenging the parents' authority by refusing to comply with a command or rule.[2] It's when we say, "Tommy, go clean up your room" and he replies, "No, I won't." Tommy is saying, "I want to be in control."

Dr. Bruce Narramore says, "Even though we force the right behavior from the child, he has manipulated our feelings to the point of anger, fear, or frustration. To a child, this is victory. Whenever a child makes us lose our temper, he has won a victory."[3]

Dr. Narramore also gives us three ways to determine if we are in a power struggle:

1. Our attitude: Whenever we feel angry or frustrated, we are in a power struggle, no matter what we do!
2. Tone of voice: Although we convince ourselves of pure motives and calm attitude, our voice gives us away.
3. Our child's reactions: When a child is stubborn or negative over a period of time, we are involved in a struggle for power.[4]

We can stay out of the power struggle by realizing we don't need to prove our authority, we only need to exercise it. We do that by disciplining correctly, and thus not becoming upset or angry.

The problem is that when a child asks, "Who's in power here?" we get frightened. We're not sure. Our insecurity then causes us to take up our child's challenge and try to prove we are in power, that we are the authority.

Some Valuable Differences

We don't need to prove it, because it is a fact based on God's provision, regardless of what our child thinks. Ephesians 6:1,2a says, "Children, obey your parents; this is the right thing to do because God has placed them in authority over you. Honor your father and mother" (LB).

We can be secure, knowing that God has given us authority as parents. Our child cannot take that away from us. We may think he has sometimes, but in principle, it is always ours. Therefore, we don't need to feel threatened. We can exercise our authority confidently and calmly. In the next two chapters, we will learn how to do that as we examine six different methods of discipline.

WHAT YOU CAN DO

1. Make sure you instruct and train your child before you correct him.
2. Think back over several of your child's acts of misbehavior and identify them as willfull disobedience or childish responsibility. Determine how you will respond the next time he or she has an accident or disobeys.

Chapter 14

Discipline Starts with Communication

Jody writes, "I can't control my kids, especially my seven-year-old. I have to get after him all the time. He doesn't listen to me. Every morning before school, he starts to play and I have to talk to him three or four times. Then I threaten him, but he doesn't care. I get so mad because I have to talk to him over and over again."

Jody has a communication problem. She's talking, but her son isn't listening. Because he's not listening, he's not obeying.

Obedience always starts with communication; it is foundational for effective discipline. Jody needs to learn not only to communicate (which we'll cover in this chapter), but also to back up her talk with action (which is our topic in chapter 15).

Healing the Angry Heart

In considering communication, we must think about the words we use. Do you remember the example I used in the section on stress about a father and his small daughter who were walking through the woods? The father said "Stay on the path," but the little girl didn't know what a path was; how could she stay on it? That story clearly demonstrates how we assume our children understand us, when actually, they may not. Sometimes we even assume they can read our minds.

Here are some ways to make sure that our communication reaches our children:

First, *stand close to them while giving instructions*. It's hard to communicate when we're yelling from the other room. Instead, we need to have eye contact. We also should have them repeat the instruction back to us so we know they hear us.

Second, *don't say more than twelve words at a time in giving instructions*. I have a bad habit of giving Darcy, all at once, a list of things to do. "First, go clean your room, then come set the table, and don't forget to do your homework before you go to bed." How silly! By the time I get to the last command, she's forgotten the first one. So I'm learning to give her one duty at a time. After the first one is completed, I give the next direction. I also praise her when a task is completed.

Third, *be specific in our commands and rules*. H. Norman Wright explains that a specific rule lets the other person know exactly what you mean and lets him know instantly when he has broken it.[1]

We can be specific by breaking the command down into steps. For instance, we could say, "Picking up toys means taking this block and putting it with the other blocks. Now take this car and put it in your toy box," etc.

If you want to know how you're doing on these three

objectives, tape record your interaction with your family. You may be surprised to find out how many words you actually say and whether or not you are specific.

TRAINING IN MISBEHAVIOR?

As you listen to the tape, count the number of positive responses and negative responses you give your child. Cultivate the habit of giving more positive input than negative.

I must confess I often find myself so busy that I pay attention to my children only when they misbehave. Then I must stop in my tracks and remind myself to give them some positive attention.

Our children learn to use their strong negative behavior to get the attention they *need* when we ignore their more subtle, quiet, good behavior and fail to give them the attention they *deserve*. In a sense, we train them to misbehave when we pay attention only to their wrongdoing. Instead, we should be more aware of our interactions with them and determine to give them more positive than negative responses.

Heather's psychologist instructed her to make a point of sincerely praising her children every five or ten minutes. She believes it strengthened her children's desire for good behavior. She found out how much they wanted to please her and gain her approval.

COMMAND OR REQUEST?

As we look at communicating with our children, we also need to distinguish between giving a command and making a request. A command is a directive that must be obeyed. A request gives a child a choice whether or not to do something.

If I want Darcy to obey me, I should not say, "Are you ready to clean your room?" or "Would you clean your room?" When she answers, "No," I think she is disobeying me. In reality she isn't; she is answering my question truthfully. I meant it to be a command, but it was a request.

When we give a command, we still can say "please" and talk courteously. We can say, "Please clean your room now."

By stating our desires in a command, using a courteous tone of voice, we will make our child feel secure. He'll know he doesn't have a choice and should obey our command.

We have considered some important points about communication, the foundation for effective discipline. The next chapter will give us five more methods.

WHAT YOU CAN DO

1. For three days, keep a list of every positive and negative response you give your child. Then begin to concentrate on praising your child more than you criticize him.

2. If you want your child to do something, without giving him a choice, state it as a command instead of a request.

Chapter 15

Methods of Discipline

Several methods of discipline are available for our children's various stages of development. First, wc'll cover spanking since it is used with young children, and then we'll see some other avenues we can use.

SPANKING

Julie rounded the corner of her living room and stopped short. Two-year-old Danny was sitting on the carpet beside a philodendron and its empty pot, sifting its soil and bits of roots through his fingers.

"Danny!" shouted Julie. "How many times have I told you not to play in the soil!" She reached him in two steps, jerked him up by his arm and began hitting his bottom and upper legs with her hand. It wasn't until all her angry tension was unleashed that she dropped the sobbing boy onto the floor.

Healing the Angry Heart

This kind of spanking is not effective discipline. It is not wise to spank when we're angry or under a lot of stress. We might not think we'll lose control, but spanking easily can become a release for our hidden frustration.

The best procedure I've found for controlled spanking is this seven step process, which Betty Chase developed:[1]

1. Get alone with the child; do not publicly embarrass him.
2. Ask, "What is our rule?" or "What did Daddy (or Mommy) say?" Make sure the child understood your instruction before you correct him.
3. Ask, "What did you do?" You are asking him to establish personal responsibility for his actions and to confess. This is important.
4. Explain that you love him, and equate love with correction. Say, "I love you and want to help you learn how to do the right thing next time."
5. Spank the child. Give him a few swift, but painful swats on the buttocks. The child's angry, mad cry should change to a softer, giving-in cry.
6. Comfort the child immediately after spanking him. Do not reject the child; hold him close and reassure him of your love. Only the parent who spanks should do the comforting.
7. If possible, have the child make restitution.

Following these steps will diminish the temptation to strike out in anger.

Spanking is most appropriate with a small child. As the child grows, other methods, such as the ones we'll discuss shortly, could be used.

When we spank, we need to decide whether to use our hands or an object to spank with. I found that the few extra minutes it took to get the wooden spoon from the kitchen gave me an opportunity to compose myself. By the time I returned to Darcy with the spoon, I had decided how I would talk to her. I could then spank her in love and instruction. Sometimes, before getting back to Darcy, I broke the spoon in half with the frustration that I otherwise would have unleashed on her. Breaking the spoon vented the anger that wanted to hurt Darcy, and dropping the pieces into the trash can was a distractor for me.

Some people believe that using your hand is a good way to make sure you don't inflict injury. After all, if your hand starts to hurt, it's time to stop.

Whatever you decide is best for you, it is important to use it consistently and spank only when you're in control. If necessary, use the distractors we talked about in the anger section, or walk away. Then come back to the child and calmly go through the seven steps for spanking.

Now let's rewrite the scene between Julie and Danny. When Julie sees Danny on the floor with the soil, she could take a deep breath to slow down her natural reaction of anger. Or she could turn quickly and walk away, muttering to herself, "O.K., now, he's done that three times this week, but I've got to control myself. Consistent disciplining—not anger—is going to change him." She might even run in place for a minute to release her anger.

Then she would come back, go to the kitchen to get the paddle or wooden spoon, and when she finally reached Danny, she would be in control of herself. (She should not go to him until she is). She sits down on the couch and places him in her lap. He may see the spoon and cry, "No, Mommy, no spanking. I no do it again."

Julie says, "Yes, Danny, that's right. I'm going to help you remember not to play with the dirt. What did Mommy say about playing in the dirt?"

Danny looks at her, with tears brimming in his eyes, and replies, "No play in dirt."

"That's right, honey, and what did you do?"

Danny looks away and won't say anything, so Julie pulls his face back to hers and repeats, "What did you do wrong?"

"I play in dirt," he whispers as tears roll down his cheeks.

"Yes, you disobeyed, didn't you? What happens when you don't obey?"

Now tears are cascading down Danny's cheeks. "I no want spanking."

"I know you don't, Danny, but I have to spank you so you'll remember to obey next time. I love you, honey, and I want you to obey me and Jesus."

Julie lays Danny over her lap and gives him several swats. He cries loud at first, but then calms down. She picks Danny up and puts her arms around him for several minutes. Then Julie says, "I forgive you, Danny. Let's pick up the dirt now."

EXTINCTION AND REINFORCEMENT

Besides spanking, extinction and reinforcement are two other methods of discipline we can choose from.

Extinction is ignoring negative behavior. When the child sees that the negative behavior doesn't get him what he wants, he stops his behavior.

Reinforcement is rewarding desirable behavior. The rewards can be: social or nonsocial. Social reinforcers include hugging, talking, praising and listening. Nonsocial reinforcers are objects, such as candy, money and toys.

Sometimes, without realizing it, we reward misbehavior. Dr. Bruce Narramore explains, "Take spanking, for example. We look at spankings as a form of punishment. We wonder why some children egg us into spanking them. It doesn't make sense from our perspective. But from the viewpoint of rewards, the mystery is solved. Even though spanking is unpleasant, some children are willing to endure pain to receive the reward of parental attention. We think spankings weaken negative behavior. Actually, our increased attention may encourage future misconduct."[2] Therefore, we need to give our children plenty of positive reinforcement.

I successfully used the techniques of extinction and reinforcement to eliminate fighting between Darcy and Mark, when they were six and four years old. I told them that every time I noticed they were playing together nicely for a period of time, I would reward them each with one cookie. I ignored the times they fought, but rewarded them when they played well together.

After a while, I heard Darcy tell Mark, "Let's play nicely so we can get a cookie." Soon Darcy would call from the bedroom, "Hey, Mom, we're playing together. Can we have a cookie?" I would not give them cookies at that moment, because I had told them I had to notice their good behavior, without them asking. But within a short time, I would go in with the reward. As a result, cooperative play increased around our house.

A friend of mine applies the same principles by rewarding stars on a chart for playing nicely together. After her children earn a predetermined number of stars, they go on an outing, to an amusement park for example.

I also used these principles to correct Darcy's whining. When children whine, our usual response is to tell them to stop whining. Without realizing it, we encourage them to whine by rewarding them with attention. We compound the problem if we have difficulty immediately paying attention to their pleasant-toned conversation. Therefore, we must concentrate on responding to the favorable behavior with praise. Then we'll see a change in our children's tone of voice.

To correct Darcy's behavior, I told her that I would not listen to anything she said in a whining tone. If she had a pleasant tone of voice, I immediately paid attention to her and praised her for speaking nicely.

I added an extra part, too. When she whined, I put my hand on the top of my head to remind her I could hear her but couldn't answer because of her tone of voice. That way, she wouldn't think I couldn't hear her and whine even more loudly. At times, she burst out laughing when I put my hand on my head. That helped her change her attitude.

NATURAL CONSEQUENCES

Another method of discipline is natural consequences. This means that we simply allow nature to run its course, knowing that it will teach the child something. The story of the prodigal son (see Luke 15) illustrates this principle. The father in Jesus' parable allowed his son to suffer the natural consequences of his disobedience, and the son eventually repented.

If it had been my son who wanted to leave, I would have been tempted to warn and scold him, and not let him take any money with him. But he probably would have returned as rebellious as he was when he left. The wise father in the parable, however, received back a humbled son, who never would forget that lesson of life.

This method also works well with an under-eating child.

Natural consequences allow him to get hungry if he refuses to eat. As soon as he sees that we're not going to get upset when he doesn't eat, the challenge of the battle disappears— it's no fun to be finicky for nothing. And I can assure you, the hunger reflex that God has built into him will be a greater motivation to eat than all our interference.

Our responsibility is to allow no in-between-meal snacking or junk foods, and to provide good, well-balanced meals. Eating those meals is his responsibility.

LOGICAL CONSEQUENCES

Our final choice of disciplining methods is logical consequences. When a natural consequence is not connected with a wrong behavior, we must intervene and supply a consequence. As with natural consequences, children learn from the outcome of their misbehavior. With logical consequences, however, we structure the consequence. And as the name implies, the consequence is "logically" related to the misdeed.

Here are some examples:

1. A two-year-old child carelessly spills her milk. Logical consequence: Give her a cup that doesn't spill or that has a dripless spout.

2. A child knows how to dry dishes properly, but one evening does a sloppy job. Logical consequence: He must dry the dishes over again.

3. A five-year-old consistently leaves his toys all over the living room. Logical consequence: Remove the toys for a specific time. Each time he repeats the misbehavior, increase the time he can't play with them.

4. Maggie, age seven, is often late for school because she gets ready slowly. Logical consequence: She must go to bed thirty minutes earlier at night or wake up thirty minutes earlier in the morning. In both cases, if she's still late for school, allow her to suffer the consequences determined by the school.

5. Two-year-old Brian continually runs out into the street after being instructed not to. Logical consequence: He must play in the house or back yard for a specified

143

amount of time.

6. Three-year-old Mark screams at the table if the food isn't served fast enough or if it's not what he wanted. Logical consequence: Take him to his bedroom to stay until he stops crying and can be happy at the table. Remove him from the table immediately each time he starts to cry.

7. Susie fights with the neighborhood children when they come to play at her house. Logical consequence: Have the neighborhood children leave for a specified amount of time.

The logical consequences method of discipline is one of the most effective. It eliminates the power struggles that ensue when we try to force children to do something. It also teaches children responsibility for their own actions and decisions. We can have difficulty using logical consequences, though, because it is hard to remove ourselves from the situations and allow our children to learn the lessons. We must come to the point of letting our children take responsibility for their behavior. We must realize that we make things worse when we interfere, but we help them mature if we stay out of it.

Although logical consequences work best with a child who can understand the cause and effect principle, they also can be used with a younger child. For instance, if he doesn't use a toy properly, remove it for a while. If he throws food at a meal, excuse him from the table. If he has a temper tantrum, calmly put him in another room and close the door, or remove yourself from his sight. (A temper tantrum isn't any fun without an audience).

Disciplining children is not an easy, once-a-day-and-then-they-will-be-perfect kind of task. It is a continual, sometimes wearying job that requires our strength and dependence upon God.

But there are some encouraging times. Besides, we also are growing through the process. As we help them mature, God teaches us to mature and grow more like His loving Son, Jesus. They are hard lessons for them and for us. But as God breaks and molds us and our children, He puts us back together again, without the weak parts.

We're all like rough diamonds, whose uneven edges must be chipped away to reveal the beauty and reflection of Jesus underneath. We and our children are also like the clay that this poem speaks of:

A PIECE OF CLAY

I took a piece of plastic clay
   And idly fashioned it one day,
And as my fingers pressed it still,
   It moved and yielded to my will.

I came again when days were past:
   The feel of clay was hard at last.
The form I gave it, it still bore,
   But I could change that form no more.

I took a piece of living clay
   And gently formed it day by day
And moulded with my press and art
   A young child's soft and yielding heart.

I came again when years were gone:
   It was a man I looked upon.
He still that early impress wore,
And I could change it never more.

                Anonymous

Healing the Angry Heart

WHAT YOU CAN DO

1. Write down several of your child's different acts of disobedience and determine which method of discipline you consistently and immediately will use for each one.
2. Write on a card the seven steps for spanking. Decide where in your home you will take your child for a spanking, and post the card there. Spank only in that area and follow the seven steps.

Section V

Rebuild Yourself and Your Child

Chapter 16

Forgive But Don't Forget

June had been crying even before she reached me on the telephone. The mother of a twelve-year-old boy, she has been deeply depressed for almost nine months thinking about how she abused her son when he was younger. She is concerned about the scars he might be carrying around inside him, which could surface later. Her depression prevents her from thinking positively about the future. She dwells only on the past and how she acted.

"When I send him off to school in the morning," she told me, "I can't keep from crying. During the day, I see his pained face as a little boy, when I screamed at him incessantly for the childish things he did. I yelled at him about the wrinkles in his bed after he made it. I berated him for spilling papers when he took out the trash. I know I am a perfectionist, but I can't seem

149

to stop reacting angrily. We seem to have a fairly good relationship now; we even play tennis and do other things together. But all I can think about is what I've done to him."

June can't forgive herself for what she has done. As a result, she has no hope for the future and is in deep depression. She continues to punish herself, thinking that she doesn't deserve forgiveness. As a result, she is not doing the good things she could do today to build up her child for the future. And today is tomorrow's regret or praise.

When we feel as June does, we need hope for the future. We need hope that we can forgive ourselves for the past and hope that our child will grow into a normal adult.

FORGIVE YOURSELF

This chapter is entitled "Forgive But Don't Forget" because I want to encourage you to forgive yourself for the past, but not to forget it. You *can* forgive yourself, but you *can't* forget the past. Only God can forget. But you can stop dwelling on the *pain of the past*.

This can be a long process, but it begins with forgiving ourselves. James W. Angell says, "We can't change the past, but we have a lot to say about the attitude we take toward it."[1]

What does forgive mean? The dictionary defines forgiveness as "giving up resentment against, giving up wanting to punish, stop being angry, a pardon." Pardon is defined as "to release from punishment, to cancel or not exact a penalty, to overlook."

Therefore, when we forgive ourselves, we don't try to punish ourselves any more. We stop being angry at ourselves. We no longer dwell on how terrible we were. *We overlook the past by pounding a big, red "FORGIVEN" stamp on it.*

In order to forgive ourselves, we need to remember three things. The first is why we have the right to forgive ourselves.

We do because God already forgave us when we accepted Christ as our Savior. (If you haven't done that yet, see chapter 5). Jesus already paid the penalty for our sin, so we don't have to. We simply need to acknowledge our wrongdoing and ask for forgiveness, based on 1 John 1:9, which says: "If we confess our sins, He is faithful and righteous to forgive us our sins and to cleanse us from all unrighteousness." Then we can forgive ourselves.

Second, God wants to forgive us so much more than we can comprehend. He wants us to be cleansed so that we can live in the power of Christ. He knows that is the only way we can live the victorious Christian life.

God also wants to forgive us for *His own sake*. Isaiah 43:25 says, "I, even I, am He that blotteth out thy transgressions for Mine own sake, and will not remember thy sins" (KJV). He wants, desires, *yearns* for fellowship with us. He can have fellowship with us only if we are clean and free from sin. Therefore, His longing for a relationship with each of us motivates Him to want to forgive us.

If we could grasp His strong desire for fellowship, we would know without a doubt that He doesn't want to punish us. He wants to release us from punishment for His own sake.

Third, God—and only God—can forgive *and forget*. We have difficulty understanding that because we don't forgive ourselves. Yet, when we say, "Lord, I did it again. Please forgive me, again!" He says, "Did you do that before? I don't remember, but I'll be glad to forgive you."

We rehash our angry reactions over and over in our minds, but God forgets. Psalm 103:12 says, "As far as the east is from the west, so far has He removed our transgressions from us."

STEPS TO FORGIVING YOURSELF

If you have difficulty forgiving yourself, follow these

Healing the Angry Heart

four steps:

1. *See the value of forgiving yourself.* If you can see that punishing yourself doesn't do you or anyone else any good, then you can understand the value of forgiving yourself. I can best illustrate this contrast with the following chart:

PUNISHING YOURSELF	FORGIVING YOURSELF
1. breaks your relationship with God	1. restores your relationship with God
2. produces absence of Holy Spirit's power therefore weakness in resisting temptation	2. allows presence of Holy Spirit's power, giving strength to resist next anger temptation
3. focuses only on self	3. allows focus on others
4. destroys freedom to love and accept others, especially children	4. frees you to love and accept others, especially children
5. does not change past	5. changes present and prepares for future
6. results in bitterness, self-hatred, depression	6. results in abundant living, joy, service for God

2. *Make a decision with your will.* Decide to forgive yourself, even though you don't feel like it. Say something like, "Heavenly Father, thank You that Jesus died on the cross so that I don't have to pay the penalty for my own sins. I know You want me to forgive myself so I can have fellowship with You. I don't feel that I want to, Lord, but with Your power, I choose to forgive myself. I ask You to make this real in my life."

152

You may not sense any immediate change in your attitudes, which is why you need to proceed to step three.

3. *Breathe spiritually every time Satan reminds you of your past.* Spiritual breathing is:

Exhaling: confessing present sin or, in the case of remembering an already forgiven sin, rejecting negative thoughts such as "How can God possibly forgive me for what I've done to my child?"

Inhaling: receiving God's forgiveness by faith, or reminding yourself that you are forgiven and deciding not to punish yourself any longer.

Now you really will be able to tell if your revised self-talk is successful. When Satan sends darts saying, "My child will be scarred for life," or "Why did I act like that?" or "I'm a horrible mother to have done that," you can remind him that you are forgiven and God has forgotten.

Spiritual breathing involves a commitment to exhale sin and inhale forgiveness time and time again. Sometimes it is wearying, but eventually the pain of the past will diminish. It will become easier to forgive yourself.

4. *Tell someone else.* Telling someone else will cement your decision in your mind. You don't have to give a long explanation; just say, "I need to tell someone that I have forgiven myself." If you can go into more detail, that's even better. Ask your friend to pray for you, and keep her informed as to your progress.

You may wonder why I am so confident that you can forgive yourself. It is because *I've* forgiven *myself.* It wasn't a one-time choice, though. Just like growth, it was a process of becoming more comfortable and forgiving myself and fighting off my unhealthy thoughts about what I'd done. Little by little, I stopped punishing myself and started sensing

Healing the Angry Heart

God's love. Forgiveness and the passage of time diminished the pain of my past. That freed me to share with others and help them.

You can experience that same progress. Begin by seeing the value of forgiving yourself.

DON'T FORGET THE PAST

While we want to lessen the pain of the past, we don't want to forget it. There are several reasons for this.

First, remembering our past sins can keep us humble. It should *not* give us a poor self-image, but it *should* cause us to keep our eyes on Jesus. It should encourage us to depend upon Him instead of our own self-sufficiency. As a result, we'll grow in our Christian maturity.

Second, we'll have more compassion for others, especially for those who are going through similar struggles. Rather than thinking, *I'm shocked that she could be doing that!* we'll think, *I'm so sorry to hear she's having that problem. Maybe what helped me can help her. I'll share it with her.*

That is the third reason not to forget the past: so that we can share with others. Second Corinthians 1:3,4 says, "What a wonderful God we have—He is the Father of our Lord Jesus Christ, the source of every mercy, and the one who so wonderfully comforts and strengthens us in our hardships and trials. And why does He do this? So that when others are troubled, needing our sympathy and encouragement, we can pass on to them this same help and comfort God has given us" (LB). As God uses us to help others, we, too, will benefit, because our self-image will become healthier.

Finally, God will be glorified as we share with others the healing work that He has done in our lives. He will receive the glory and praise.

Erica knows these four reasons for not forgetting those

times when she abused her two daughters. Through counseling, she painfully discovered the many causes of her uncontrollable anger. Yet, even though she learned control, she was afraid to tell anyone about her experience.

Eventually, as she forgave herself and as the pain of the past diminished, she was so excited about what God did in her life that she mentioned it to a friend. It turned out that her friend was abusing her son and was terrified that someone might find out. The friend told Erica that Erica's sharing helped her. Erica became encouraged and told more people over a period of time, and she never received a negative response.

During the time that Erica hurt her daughters, she thought, "Romans 8:28 can't be true. God certainly can't use this for good." Now she knows it *is* true. She has helped others, and God has been glorified.

She says, "God is creative and He can use anything when we allow Him to work in us. I thought I was the only Christian who abused her child. Now I come into contact with many who are struggling with their anger. Often I've helped them and that's a joy. Nothing is as wonderful as ministering in the name of Jesus!"

WHAT YOU CAN DO

1. Identify at least one good result of your painful past.
2. Memorize Jeremiah 29:11: " 'For I know the plans that I have for you,' declares the Lord, 'plans for welfare and not for calamity to give you a future and a hope.' "

Chapter 17

Healing the Relationship

"I guess I am most grieved about the past two years, because 'they' say the first years are the most important in a child's life. How I wish I could redo the time from when Joshua was eighteen months old until now. Did you ever feel this way? My heart is so sad because I love him so much and deeply regret my ugliness and hatefulness.

"Often as I think about it, I get angry at God because I never knew I would be so angry as a parent. Is Joshua's psychological damage irreversible? I wonder how my verbal abuse has affected him, and I feel so guilty that I've blown these formative years. My biggest fear to this day is that I won't raise my two boys in a way that pleases the Lord.

"When Joshua was first born, I remember crying for several days about my awesome responsibility to raise him as God would have me. The depth of my love was unceasing, and I didn't have any intentions of becoming angry. But the past two years are history now. I continually am asking God for wisdom beyond my years. I hate to fail my children. People say I'm too hard on myself, but I have to be concerned so I will do the best job I can."

Doris' letter represents the feelings of many of us. We are awed at the responsibility of being parents. We want to be the best mothers in the world. We never intended to become angry, and now that we think we've damaged our child, either physically or emotionally, we wonder if the harm can be reversed.

When we feel this way, we need to believe that God can heal our relationships with our children. We also need to take positive steps toward building the self-esteem of our children.

Healing the relationship starts with believing God for His renewing powers and then going on to gain the child's trust. We will cover those topics in this chapter. In the next, we'll look at practical ways to build our child's self-esteem.

GOD'S PROMISES FOR HEALING

We learned in the previous chapter how much God yearns to forgive us and to help us forgive ourselves. He desires just as strongly to rebuild the relationship between us and our children. He promises us, "Do not call to mind the former things, or ponder things of the past. Behold, I will do something new, now it will spring forth; will you not be aware of it? I will even make a roadway in the wilderness, rivers in the desert" (Isaiah 43:18,19).

Does it seem as if a stark desert of unlove, maybe even hate, lies between you and your child? That's how I felt when I couldn't control my temper with Darcy. I feared that we might never have a good relationship. But God has since given

Darcy and me rivers of love in that desert.

He can do the same for you. Will you "be aware" of it? You can watch for it expectantly. Just as a new river flowing through a desert causes seeds to sprout, God will nurture little sprouts of love and care in your relationship. Yes, you still may see times of aridity, but keep looking for God's miracle. He wants to heal your relationship, to the praise of His name.

Just like Doris, you may wonder if the months or years of yelling at your child or physically abusing him are irreversible. How can God do anything about the past? God assures us, "Then I will make up to you for the years that the swarming locust has eaten, the creeping locust, the stripping locust, and the gnawing locust, my great arm which I sent among you. And you shall have plenty to eat and be satisfied, and praise the name of the Lord your God, Who has dealt wondrously with you; then My people will never be put to shame" (Joel 2:25,26).

Maybe my paraphrase will make this promise more clear. "Then I will make up to you for the times you yelled at your children or hit them or spanked them in anger or cursed at them or didn't give them the love they needed. In time, you will be satisfied with the way you are treating them, and you will praise the Lord, who empowered you to change. Then other people will respect your parenting choices."

Charles R. Swindoll comments on this passage of Scripture saying, "If He was able to 'make up for the years' locusts devoured the crops of Judah, then He is certainly able to do the same for you with your family—even though it may seem impossible. God is a specialist in impossible situations. He is the physician who can bring internal healing. He specializes in binding up fractured relationships and healing deep wounds and bruises that have existed for years."[1]

159

God is the God of the Impossible. The more impossible the situation seems, the more glory He receives from it, because no man could have accomplished it. God is also creative and can help you understand your child's needs.

UNDERSTANDING THE ABUSED OR NEGLECTED CHILD

Before we can start to repair the damaged relationship with our child, we need to understand how he may be looking at his world. Recognizing how he thinks and feels can help us meet his needs.

Abused children generally have some of these characteristics:

1. The abused child has a *distorted view of love*. He equates love with the attention he gets. Most of the time, that attention is negative and painful, but it is still attention, and it is the only love he knows. It is the way of interaction most familiar to him and he wants it to continue.

2. The abused child has *low self-esteem and low self-image*. He doesn't like himself or believe that he is a valuable human being. Nor does he believe that he is worthy of love. These feelings may have come from being called names, being labeled as "bad" or being physically battered. Regardless, he doesn't believe that he can contribute anything to this world.

Just as he may think of himself as "all bad," he thinks of his parents as "all good." After all, how can he criticize his parents—they are the adults, the authority? He reasons that it must be his problem, his fault that they inflict all the pain and hurt on him.

3. The abused child *protects himself in an effort to survive*. He may do this by being passive or being aggressive.

Not wanting or needing anything protects him from being

160

rejected or hurt. If he doesn't speak, he may not get beaten. If he is good as he can be, he won't make his parents angry and abusive. If he doesn't expect anything, he won't be disappointed.

Or he may react with hostility. He thinks that having the attitude of "nothing can hurt me, I'm tough" will protect him from emotional pain.

4. The abused child *keeps himself isolated.* Playing by himself, he believes that he is less likely to make anyone angry or to be rejected. When he does find a friend, however, he sometimes will latch onto that person and require more love and attention than the person possibly can give. If the friend then rejects him, it reinforces the child's view of himself as unworthy of love.

5. The abused child *handles success destructively.* He either is not satisfied when he reaches a goal or he doesn't try at all. He either feels pressured to outperform everyone else or he doesn't take any risks. These extreme reactions make it almost impossible for him to feel happy with himself for accomplishing something.

These five characteristics help us understand the abused child. As a result of his viewpoint, he lacks trust in his relationship with us. Now we can go on to heal that injured relationship by restoring his confidence in our love.

BE UNIFIED

In abusive families, parents often are at odds with each other, and the child gains control by manipulating the parents against each other. If the parents recognize this and stand firmly together in their decisions, the child begins to trust them.

To convey a sense of unity, the parents should talk over decisions in a room separate from the child. If they discuss their problems loudly, they should explain later that they don't hate each other.

John and Evie realized that their son, Brant, had been pitting them against each other because their own relationship was rocky. Brant would go to one parent with a request. If he was refused, he went to the more liberal parent, usually Evie, with the same request and whined until she relented. When John found out Evie had given in to Brant, he exploded and verbally abused her for being weak and gullible.

As John and Evie began to repair their marriage, they recognized Brant's tactics. Now, they consult each other and ask Brant, "What did your father (or mother) say?" Often they talk to the other person before making a decision.

Brant began to see that he couldn't control his parents, so he started to feel better about himself. You see, Brant was afraid that he actually was causing their potential divorce, so he experienced tremendous guilt. Even though a part of him wanted them to fight, he eventually felt relieved when they became united.

Parents also can be unified by not taking their problems to the child. When Alice felt disgusted with her husband, she often turned to her eight-year-old daughter, Tammy, as a sounding board. Tammy also had a shoulder for Alice to cry on when she couldn't communicate with her husband. But when her husband treated her well, Alice rejected her daughter's hugs and comfort. The constant change in her mother confused Tammy, and then she disobeyed to get her mother's attention. Eventually, as a result of counseling, Alice understood that she was expecting Tammy to fulfill an adult role. She learned to communicate her needs to her husband, and Tammy became a daughter instead of a confidant.

BE HONEST

Parents also can develop trust in their child by honestly sharing their feelings and by meaning what they say. Joyce struggled with abusive anger toward her son, Art, and gave him conflicting messages. At times when she was angry but was trying to repress her anger, she smiled, yet her voice was filled with hate and anger. Later, when stress overwhelmed her, she exploded with the suppressed anger. Art never knew whether a smile meant approval or eventual punishment.

In a parenting class, Joyce learned to acknowledge and not repress her anger. She also learned to express "I" messages instead of "you" messages. As a result, she separated Art's actions from who he is. She honestly shared her feelings, but said, "I don't like . . . ," rather than "You are. . . ."

"I" messages, such as "I don't like . . ." or "I feel . . .," are constructive ways to express yourself. "You" messages are destructive, as they put the child down for who he is. "You are stupid," or "Look at the stupid thing you did" concentrate on who the child is—he is stupid. "You make me angry" puts the responsibility for our reactions on him, rather than on us.

Another way to be honest is to ask for our child's forgiveness for the hurt we've caused him. We also can reassure him that it is our problem, not his. We may need to tell him again and again that he is valuable and worthy of love. We'll need to demonstrate it as well, by practicing the suggestions in this book.

BE CONSISTENT

Finally, we can develop trust by being consistent in disciplining our child. This may be difficult, because the abused child will test us to see if we will hold to this new "program." He will disobey in greater and greater ways until he is convinced that we will stick to the limits we've set. His negative reactions may surprise us, because when we "get our act together," we expect our child to respond positively immediately. Instead, he may egg us on.

He resists because the "new program" threatens him. It is unfamiliar and he doesn't know his "place." He would rather have the old, familiar abuse, even though it is painful. He's insecure because we haven't acted consistently in the past. He didn't know if his crying would get our sympathy or our wrath. Now he still isn't sure how we'll react.

If we understand his insecurity, we'll be better able to cope and be patient. We can give him time to learn that we are committed to being consistent and patient. His reactions are not negative comments on us personally. They also don't mean that our new techniques will not work.

As we continue to respond consistently, despite his in security, we'll be far along toward instilling trust and a correct sense of what love is. We will add a new trust to his concept of our parent-child relationship, and eventually he'll respond with love.

SEEK COUNSELING

To fully develop your child's trust, you may need to seek professional Christian counseling for him and yourselves. Nothing is "unspiritual" or "weak" about such a decision. A professional who understands how people react can help you and your child solve the underlying problems and strengthen your relationship.

Also, your child may share his feelings more freely with an objective observer. He then can deal with his own love/hate sensations better than if he can't tell you for fear of hurting you.

Finally, a professional counselor can give both of you insights and practical ideas for healing the wounds.

Healing the Relationship

Please seek this kind of help if you think there is any possibility that you need it. You won't be sorry.

WHAT YOU CAN DO

Consider these scriptural promises and determine which you will claim and memorize: Isaiah 43:18,19 or Joel 2:25,26.

Chapter 18
Boost Your Child's Self-Esteem

At the beginning of this book, we looked at our own self-images. Now that we are drawing to a close, it's appropriate to concentrate on our children's self-images. Boosting their self-esteem is a big part of rebuilding our relationships with them. Therefore, we will explore some areas that will help us build up our children.

LOVING BY FAITH

At times do you wonder if you truly love your child? Do you wonder how you can build him up when you don't even like him?

If you sometimes feel love for your child and at other times think you hate him, you are experiencing something very natural. You are having *ambivalent feelings.*

Ambivalence is defined as "simultaneous conflicting

feelings toward a person or thing, as love and hate." Because I experienced both love and hate toward Darcy as she was growing up, and especially when she was a toddler, I wondered if I truly loved her. I thought my "hateful" feelings ruled out the possibility that I loved her. I didn't think love and hate could exist side by side. When I heard about ambivalent feelings, I was comforted and reassured to know that love can co-exist with unloving feelings.

As a result, I began to understand that love is more than feelings. *Love is a choice, a decision that each of us makes. And in loving others, we must love by faith.* We must choose for the highest good of another person, even though we may not "feel loving."

Krista, a mother of two teenaged girls, is struggling to rebuild her relationship with her oldest daughter, whom she abused. She told Shanna that she hated her, and she sensed a release from saying it. But she also realized that it did not help their relationship. So she then told Shanna, "Yes, I do feel like I hate you sometimes, but it is not because of you, it's because of what you do. I don't hate you. I really do care about you."

She says she knows that she cares for her, because if someone else hurts Shanna, she aches also. Even though she still doesn't feel pained when she hurts Shanna until afterwards, she realizes she slowly is developing "loving" feelings, which are evidence of her love.

We all must go through this struggle. We want to love our children, but because the things they do upset us or make them "unlovely" to us, we have difficulty feeling love toward them.

Therefore, we need to love by faith. We need to decide to love, as a matter of our will, not of our emotions. When we choose the best for our child, eventually the "feelings" of love will follow.

The very fact that you are reading this book suggests that you really love and care for your child. Otherwise you would not be interested in improving your relationship with him. So take heart. When you have those feelings of "hate," just realize that you also love, and that love is a matter of making the choices that are to your child's benefit.

EMOTIONAL TANK

The primary way to develop a strong relationship with your child is to convey love to him and thus boost his self-esteem. Yet, how can you know if you truly are making your child "feel loved?"

Dr. Ross Campbell answers this in his book, *How To Really Love Your Child*. He says that every child has "an *emotional tank*. This tank is figurative, of course, but very real. Each child has certain emotional needs, and whether these emotional needs are met (through love, understanding, discipline, etc.) determines many things. First of all, how a child feels: whether he is content, angry, depressed, or joyful. Secondly, it affects his behavior: whether he is obedient, disobedient, whiny, perky, playful, or withdrawn. Naturally, the fuller the tank, the more positive the feelings and the better the behavior."[1]

You can determine if a child is feeling loved by looking at his behavior. When a child's emotional tank lacks the "fuel" of love and self-respect, he responds by asking his parent, "Do you love me?' He doesn't ask this in words; he asks through his behavior. If you can recognize when your child is asking for the reassurance of your love or the attention he needs, you will be taking the first step toward rebuilding the love-bond. You also will be heading off disciplinary problems.

Dr. Campbell suggests using the question, "What does this child need?" instead of "What can I do to correct this child's behavior?" In effect, "Does his emotional tank need filling?" We also need to take into account the child's physical needs: Is he hungry, tired, sick or in pain?

When Darcy was six years old, I saw these principles save a confrontation and build up Darcy. She was complaining about having to clean her room. At first I became increasingly irritated at her grumpiness. But then I thought, *Maybe she's not feeling good about herself.*

I asked her if she would like to sit in the rocking chair with me. A little surprised when she agreed, I lifted her into my lap and we rocked back and forth, the rocking chair squeaking softly. We talked for twenty minutes, and little by little her grumpiness turned into happiness.

Finally, I asked her, "Would you like me to tell you the first thing to do in your room?"

Before I even finished my sentence, Darcy jumped out of my lap and walked straight to her room. She cleaned it up, needing little help.

I was amazed. Twenty minutes of love and attention had turned her from a sour-faced, unhappy complainer into my wanting-to-please little girl.

A good way to be aware of a child's emotional tank and feelings is to try to empathize with him. One day, when Mark was four-years-old, he whined about putting on his pajamas. I sensed frustration tightening my chest. "Mark," I blurted out, "I know you're tired, but put on your pajamas anyway." *Why can't he just cooperate and do it?*

Then I remembered the day before, when I had felt so tired and irritable that I just wanted to climb into bed and go to sleep. *I bet that's how tired Mark feels right now. No wonder he doesn't have enough energy to do anything.*

My frustration subsided when I empathized with him. My

tolerance level grew as I identified with his feeling. I started to help him put on his pajamas.

The next time your child disobeys or acts unlovingly, reflect back over the past couple of hours, or even days, and see if he has received the love and attention he needs. Maybe he's feeling insecure and unloved. Or maybe he's hurting emotionally because of a feeling of failure or some other negative situation. At times like that, he's asking for your reassurance about his worth and for your love.

Once we understand that a child has an emotional tank, we can use several ways to fill it. The first is nonverbal communication.

NONVERBAL COMMUNICATION

Nonverbal communication is anything we do without words that reveals something. It can be either positive or negative. Dr. Campbell believes that three methods of nonverbal communication—eye contact, physical contact and focused attention—are the main ways to convey love. First, let's talk about eye contact.

Have you ever talked with someone who won't look you in the eyes as you converse? It is distracting, isn't it? You may even begin to wonder if he cares about what you are saying.

It is the same with our children. We need to look into their eyes more often than just when we want to give them instructions. Looking at them shows that we are interested in them and makes them feel good about themselves. "Bright eyes [the light of the eyes] gladden the heart" (Proverbs 15:30).

Be aware, though, that we can look at our children and not really be "there." They know when our thoughts are elsewhere. Keeping our eyes *and* our attention on our children will build their confidence and self-esteem.

Healing the Angry Heart

After recognizing the importance of eye contact, I have tried to make a point of looking at Darcy and Mark when they speak to me or I talk to them. This is more difficult than it sounds because usually my hands are busy and I need to watch what I'm doing, lest I cut myself while chopping vegetables. So, often, I must stop what I'm doing to focus on them.

Another aspect of nonverbal communication is physical contact. This includes more than hugging and kissing; it refers to any message of love we give them that involves touching physically. It might mean an arm around the shoulders, tousling the hair, holding hands while walking, holding the child in our lap, a hug while praising him or a pat on the head.

We should give these reassurances of love all the time, not just when the child does something we approve of. For instance, this narrative was printed in the Parents Anonymous' newsletter, *The Family Advocate:* "One evening as my 10-year-old son sat reading, I walked over and hugged him. My son looked up at me and said, 'Why don't you ever hug me when I'm watching TV?' I thought about my son's comment and realized that I was responding not to him but to what he was doing. All this time I thought I was giving him 'unconditional' love and was not aware of my own limitations in fulfilling this ideal."[2]

It is much more difficult to express our love with physical contact, or any other nonverbal communication, when we're upset with our children or they are doing something that displeases us. But how much more love—unconditional love—we'll convey if we use physical contact even when we are correcting or teaching them.

Darcy loves to have her back tickled, but doing that is often a decision of love, especially if I'm feeling depressed or I'm deep in thought about something. But when I make that choice and love her by faith, the contentment on her face makes me glad I did.

The third method of nonverbal communication, focused attention, is even harder to do, because it requires more time and planning. Dr. Campbell defines focused attention as that which gives "a child our full, undivided attention in such a way that he feels without doubt that he is completely loved. That he is valuable enough *in his own right* to warrant parents' undistracted watchfulness, appreciation, and uncompromising regard. In short, focused attention makes a child feel he is the most important person in the world in his parents' eyes."[3]

My most difficult decisions each day are whether or not to pay attention to my children. My interests and goals seem more important than they do, so it is a constant battle for me to give my children the attention they need. I must continually remind myself that they are more important than my household duties or outside activities, which offer more immediate rewards. The reward of seeing my children grow up with healthy self-images is more important than always having the dishes washed or a list of phone calls made (or this chapter typed).

Although this is a continual struggle, I am encouraged as I see progress. When Darcy comes home from school, we sit down together and talk over her day while she has a snack. At times, this commitment has slipped, as I might be busy or she is eager to go outside to play, but then we always return to it, and I'm grateful.

The best way to ensure that we give focused attention is to set aside time to spend with each child alone. Here are some suggestions for how to do that:

1. Mark off a block of time on your schedule, even fifteen or twenty minutes, that will be your child's special time. This

can be daily or weekly.

2. Pick up your child from school and do something together. Once a month I take each of my children out for lunch after picking them up from school.

3. Allow your child to stay up thirty minutes after his regular bedtime one night a week. He can choose whatever he wants to do with you. This is particularly effective when you have more than one child. Usually, the other children will not complain when one child stays up if they know they will get their turn.

4. Watch for unexpected opportunities. For instance, if you are waiting for the TV repairman to come, sit down and play a game with your child. Or, as you stand in a long line at the supermarket, hold your child and talk eye to eye. Walking out to your car from the store, you can hold your child's hand and sing a simple song like, "Mark is my little boy, little boy, little boy. Mark is my little boy; I love him very much" (sung to the tune of "Mary Had A Little Lamb").

These primary methods of conveying love—eye contact, physical contact and focused attention—can be three large bricks for rebuilding your new, loving relationship. They will show your child how much you love him and how important he is to you, thus building his self-esteem. And they will help you obey the biblical command to "love . . . with actions and in truth" (1 John 3:18, NIV).

ALLOW EXPRESSION OF EMOTIONS

If your child were to shout, "I hate you," in a moment of rage, what would your natural reaction be? Several years ago, mine would have been to say something like, "You can't talk to me that way! You shouldn't hate your mother." But now I'm learning to let Darcy express her emotions, and I'm trying to teach her to share them appropriately.

This is another way to build the self-esteem of your children. It lets them know we respect their feelings. When children express negative feelings, we can reflect those feelings back by saying, "Yes, I understand how you could feel that way." By allowing our children to express themselves, they will grow up learning to express their feelings in constructive, healthy ways, rather than suppressing them.

When our children express themselves negatively, however, we may feel threatened, because we're afraid of our own anger. Since we haven't controlled our anger very well, we're afraid that our children will have the same problem.

If we understand that the appropriate expression of negative feelings is healthy, we won't be intimidated. Then by not putting them down for feeling angry, we can encourage our children to cope with their emotions. We can help them express themselves appropriately either verbally or physically; for instance, by telling someone or by pounding on their pillows.

Parent Effectiveness Training recommends that parents use "active listening" as a way of allowing the child to express his feelings.[4] Active listening means hearing not only the words, but the feelings behind the words. It means feeding back a response that is intellectually on target and emotionally in tune. It should not be used every time the child speaks, but for problems that warrant a "counseling session." Also, the parent should not use it to try to change the child's behavior. It is a tool for respecting the child and accepting his feelings.

Here are some examples of active listening in several different situations:

CHILD: "You don't let me go anywhere!"
PARENT: "You're feeling disappointed about missing the

skating party."

> CHILD: "I hate school. I hate my teacher."
> PARENT: "You don't think she treats you fairly."

> CHILD: "I don't want to go to the grocery store."
> PARENT: "You are bored there."

> CHILD: "I'll never finish this model airplane."
> PARENT: "You're feeling frustrated."

> CHILD: "I hate you."
> PARENT: "You are feeling angry because you can't do what you want."

Active listening requires trying to identify what the child is feeling at the time and accepting his feeling. The easiest way to accomplish this is to reply, "You are feeling . . ." and then identify what you think is his underlying feeling. Continue this exchange until he seems at peace or doesn't want to talk anymore. Often, simply knowing that we understand his feelings dissolves his angry or unpleasant emotions.

Allowing your child to express his feelings does not mean that he can use foul language or be disrespectful. And you don't need to allow him to have a screaming fit on the floor. While you can use active listening with a toddler, it works best with a child who can talk well and reason.

OTHER WAYS TO CONVEY LOVE

In this chapter, you have seen several ideas for boosting your child's self-esteem. Here are a few more ways:

1. Give him responsibility, making sure that it matches his ability.

176

2. Remember how you wanted to be treated as a child, and then treat him the same way.

3. Respect your child by taking into account his opinions and listening to his reasons, even if you don't agree. Keep an open mind before making a decision.

4. Give common courtesies, as you would with an adult.

5. Play games on his level.

6. Include the child in your projects.

7. Give your child opportunities to choose from a list of all positive options.

8. Don't talk to someone else about the previous abuse in front of the child.

9. Take time for fun.

10. Allow your child to make requests.

11. Look at life from your child's viewpoint, as expressed by Charles R. Swindoll:

My hands are small; please don't expect perfection whenever I make my bed, draw a picture, or throw a ball. My legs are short; please slow down so I can keep up with you.

My eyes have not seen the world as yours have; please let me explore safely. Don't restrict me unnecessarily.

Housework will always be there. I'm only little for a short time—please take time to explain things to me about this wonderful world, and do so willingly.

My feelings are tender; please be sensitive to my needs. Don't nag me all day long . . . treat me as you would like to be treated.

I am a special gift from God; please treasure me as God intended you to do, holding me accountable for my actions, giving me guidelines to live by, and disciplining me in a loving manner.

Healing the Angry Heart

I need your encouragement to grow. Please go easy on the criticism; remember you can criticize the things I do without criticizing me.

Please give me the freedom to make decisions concerning myself. Permit me to fail, so that I can learn from my mistakes. Then someday I'll be prepared to make the kind of decisions life requires of me.[5]

WHAT YOU CAN DO

1. Set aside a block of time each day or week for giving your child focused attention.
2. Decide on one other way that you will build your child's self-esteem.

Chapter 19
Help and Hope

Those of us who have been out of control with our anger and possibly are hurting our children, often think, *I wonder if anyone knows I'm a child abuser? What if they take my kids away from me?*

Unfortunately, the fears behind these questions prevent us from seeking the help that we need. If we could instead look at seeking help as the first step to victory, we might not be so hesitant to reach out.

I finally got the help I needed after I became fearful that I actually would permanently injure my daughter. I vaguely shared my problem with a receptive friend, which was the beginning of victory for me.

Many state laws require that a professional counselor or organization report to social services those who are abusing their children. Though a social worker may come out to visit the home, he or she won't necessarily take the child away. Withdrawing the child is not done as often as you might expect. For the child to be removed, he must be in danger in the social worker's estimation. When a child is taken, it is to protect him and give the parent an opportunity to get help.

The rest of this chapter describes many available "support systems." I hope that becoming familiar with these avenues of aid will encourage you to seek help if you need it.

I believe the very best thing you can do is make an appointment with a Christian psychologist. Your pastor or church office can refer you to one, or you can ask your local Christian radio station or Christian television program for recommendations. Making that first call is crucial, though it may be one of the most difficult things to do.

HOT LINES

Almost every city has hot lines available seven days a week, twenty-four hours a day. This may be the easiest telephone call for you, especially if you don't know anyone who can respond to your problems. You won't have to give your name if you don't want to. The people who answer hot lines are caring, sensitive, and able to help you and guide you in making the best decision. Just having someone listen can relieve a lot of tension and stress.

An important advantage of the hot line is that the person who answers will know what facilities and resources are obtainable in your area.

The hot line for Parents Anonymous is 1-800-421-0353 (outside California) or 1-800-352-0386 (California only); Child Help USA's hot line number is 1-800-422-4453. Now we will look at these two organizations.

PARENTS ANONYMOUS

Parents Anonymous is a crisis-intervention program designed to help parents prevent damaging relationships with their children. It was started in February, 1970, by a woman named Jolly K. She was 29 years old and was having trouble controlling herself with her two young daughters.

Three people attended the first meeting. Now there are more than a thousand chapters in the United States, Canada, England, Australia and on United States military bases in West Germany. Each chapter meets weekly and is conducted in an informal manner by a sponsor and chairperson. The sponsor is usually a social worker, psychologist, psychiatrist or counselor, and the chairperson is someone from the group, who acts as the leader.

As the name implies, anonymity is assured to anyone who desires it, and only first names are given at the meetings. There are no dues, and no one has to share if they don't want to.

The basic purpose of the group interaction is to give support and helpful suggestions to the members as they share their needs and concerns.

At the time I was having my problem, I was not aware of Parents Anonymous. When I began my research for this book, I discovered it and started to attend its meetings. I found that everyone there was very supportive and encouraging to me and the other members. Even more important, I saw the members experiencing success.

In dealing with our problem, we find support from others, which is what Parents Anonymous is all about. Anyone who wants to can exchange telephone numbers with another member and so they can encourage each other during the week, between meetings. A member's spouse or even a friend is always welcome at the meetings and is encouraged to come.

CHILD HELP USA

This non-profit organization was first developed in 1974 by Sara O'Meara and Yvonne Fedderson, and was named Child Help USA in 1983. It's main objective is to offer help through a hot line (1-800-422-4453) and through a Children's Village in Beaumont, California.

The Children's Village houses children who have been victims of abuse. The psychologists and other professionals there work to reunite the abusing parents with their children. They hope that this program will be a model for other "villages" to be built throughout the United States.

Every April, Child Help USA sponsors National Child Abuse Prevention Month. They distribute specially printed books on child abuse, along with other educational materials. They also conduct professional conferences.

CRISIS NURSERIES

Crisis nurseries are becoming more available as their worth is realized. Usually sponsored by the government's social services or by a volunteer organization, crisis nurseries are places where parents can bring their children when they no longer can cope or when they are in a crisis situation. This gives the parents an excellent opportunity to seek the help they need.

Many nurseries are open twenty-four hours a day and offer complete care for children ranging from newborn to five years old. They are well staffed and provide for the needs of each child. Seventy-two hours is usually the maximum time the child can be left, but that provides for parents who need a break or who don't have anyone to babysit while they go to their counseling sessions.

THE SOCIAL WORKER

The social worker is the representative of the local welfare department and its child-protection department. He or she wants to help each family in his casework, even though his is a demanding and often thankless job. Although some might fear a visit from a social worker, it can be the start of recovery. The social worker can be the "anchorperson" who reaches out and supports the parent who has no other friends or support. He can help the parent find the assistance needed, because he knows the different services available.

SOCIAL SERVICE HOMEMAKERS

One service that the social worker might suggest is the social service homemaker. This person is usually a woman, who comes into the home to help the mother learn new ways to cope with housework and child care. She may come for a few hours a day, or stay full time for several days or weeks. In a tactful and helpful manner, she might suggest different ways to organize a household to make it more efficient, or she might help in the care of the children. She is not there to take over the managing of the household, but to support and assist.

LAY THERAPISTS

A lay therapist is meant to be a friend to a parent. This relationship is not "professional," but built upon being available to do many of the ordinary things that a friend might do. For instance, he or she might provide transportation, or go shopping with the parent, or just talk on the phone. What the therapist does is primarily up to the parent. Ideally, as they spend more time together, a bond of friendship will grow between them. Often the lay therapist has the same racial and socio-economic background as the parent and thus provides the kind of encouragement that says, "I know what you're going through and I want to help."

183

PSYCHOTHERAPY

Treatment with a psychotherapist can help a parent disassociate his children from his own abusive parents. It can also help him resolve his mixed feelings toward his parents and see how his own experiences affect his relationships with his children.

This kind of therapy requires exposing the painful past, but with the help of the therapist, it can be advantageous for the patient's future.

PARENT-CHILD INTERACTION

This method allows the professional to directly observe the parent and child in a playroom situation, or possibly at mealtime and bedtime. This is helpful since the therapist is right there and able to give immediate counsel and advice. Or the sessions can be video-taped, so that the parent and therapist can discuss what happened, without the child present. Then the therapist can show the parent more appropriate ways to deal with the child. This program works best, however, after the parent has received successful and supportive treatment.

TREATMENT IN GROUPS

Group programs, such as Parents Anonymous, are successful because of the identification in the group. People find a great deal of support without a condemning attitude, since everyone is dealing with the same problem.

Group therapy can be organized exclusively for mothers, fathers or couples. Some groups are primarily educational, teaching concepts such as understanding child development and coping with the difficulties of raising children.

RESIDENTIAL TREATMENT

As the name implies, residential programs offer parents the opportunity to live with their children in a home-type situation that is closely overseen by therapists. This allows the therapists to work closely with the parents and children twenty-four hours a day. Formal parent-child interaction sessions are also included, in an effort to teach and support a better way of reacting in the family.

Some programs house the whole family, while others are limited to single mothers and their children, or to married mothers, who stay with their children while the fathers stay at home and visit the center.

Residential programs offer families immediate and intensive care and can avert a crisis that otherwise might bring harm to the family. They also have the advantage of keeping the family together, as opposed to putting the child in a foster home.

A new variation of this program places the child in a specially prepared foster home where the biological parents and the foster parents develop a cooperative relationship. Under the guidance of the National Center for the Prevention and Treatment of Child Abuse and Neglect, this new program's goal is to put the child back in the natural home within three months. This kind of a treatment is particularly beneficial because the foster parents act as surrogate parents and as models, like the lay therapists. It is hoped that a bond will form between the foster parents and the natural parents, which will become a supportive friendship.

REACH OUT FOR HELP

I want to encourage you to reach out for help in whatever way you need to. Our Heavenly Father knows we need each other, and I don't think He intends for you to try to fight the problem without human help.

Yet, it is difficult to admit our need. I often thought that asking for help would indicate that God couldn't help me, but

Healing the Angry Heart

that's not true. He has created us with needs for other people. It is not a bad testimony to seek professional assistance.

So, seek Christian professional counseling through a Christian psychologist or your pastor. In addition, find a prayer partner with whom you can share your problems several times a week. Knowing that someone else is praying specifically for you in your struggle will encourage you.

Also feel free to write me at:

P.O. Box 1058

Placentia, CA 92670

Please reach out for help. It is available, and it will give you hope.

Notes

Chapter 2, A Distortion of Christian Perfection

1. David Seamands, *Healing for Damaged Emotions*, Wheaton, IL: Victor Books, 1984, p.78.

Chapter 6, Examining Anger

1. H. Norman Wright, *The Christian Use of Emotional Power*, Old Tappan, NJ: Fleming Revell Company, 1974, p.101.
2. David Augsburger, *Be All You Can Be*, Carol Stream, IL: Creation House, 1970, p.60.
3. Theodore Isaac Rubin, *The Angry Book*, New York: The MacMillan Company, 1969, pp. 130, 131.
4. John Powell, *Why Am I Afraid To Tell You Who I Am?*

Healing the Angry Heart

Niles, IL: Argus Communications, 1969, p. 155.

5. H. Norman Wright, *Communication: Key To Your Marriage*, Glendale, CA: Regal Books, 1974, p.91.

Chapter 7, Causes of Anger

1. Theodore Isaac Rubin, *The Angry Book*, New York: The MacMillan Company, 1969, p. 153.

Chapter 9, Expectations of Perfection

1. Quoted in *To Anger With Love* by Elizabeth R. Skoglund, New York, Harper and Row, 1977, p. 69.
2. Quoted in *The Complete Toastmaster* by Herbert V. Prochnow, Englewood Cliffs, NJ: Prentice-Hall, 1960, p. 285.
3. H. Norman Wright, from "Handling Stress, Change and Depression," a seminar workbook, 1981, p. 21.
4. Taken from *Be the Woman You Want to Be* by Ruthe White, Eugene, OR: Harvest House, 1978, p. 70.
5. Quoted in "Enriched Living" seminar, by leader Verna Birkey.

Chapter 10, Over-Commitments and Time Pressures

1. Charles Swindoll, *Three Steps Forward, Two Steps Back*, Nashville: Thomas Nelson Publishers, 1980, p. 36.

Chapter 12, Hope for Depression

1. H. Norman Wright, given at seminar, "Handling Stress, Change and Depression," 1981, (May not be quoted word for word.)

Chapter 13, Some Valuable Differences

1. Bruce Narramore, *Help! I'm a Parent!* Grand Rapids, MI: Zondervan Corporation, 1972, p. 41.
2. H. Norman Wright, *Answer to Discipline,* Irvine, CA: Harvest House, 1976, p. 46.
3. Narramore, *Help!* p. 29.
4. Narramore, *Help!* pp. 30, 31.

Chapter 14, Discipline Starts With Communication

1. H. Norman Wright, *Answer to Discipline,* Irvine, CA: Harvest House, 1976, p. 39.

Chapter 15, Methods of Discipline

1. Betty Chase, *Discipline Them, Love Them,* Elgin, IL: David C. Cook Publishing, 1982, p. 28.
2. Bruce Narramore, *Help! I'm a Parent!* Grand Rapids, MI: Zondervan Corporation, 1972, p. 57.

Chapter 16, Forgive But Don't Forget

1. James W. Angell, *When God Made You, He Knew What He Was Doing,* Old Tappan, NJ: Fleming H. Revell Company, 1972, p. 150.

Chapter 17, Healing the Relationship

1. Charles R. Swindoll, *You and Your Child,* Nashville: Thomas Nelson Publishers, 1977, p. 158.

Chapter 18, Boost Your Child's Self-Esteem

1. Ross Campbell, *How To Really Love Your Child,* Wheaton, IL: Victor Books, 1977, p. 33.

Healing the Angry Heart

2. *The Family Advocate* Newsletter, July, 1980, Vol. 1, no. 2.
3. Campbell, *Really Love*, p. 55.
4. Thomas Gordon, *P.E.T. In Action,* New York: New American Library, Inc., 1975, p. 44.
5. Charles R. Swindoll, *Growing Strong in the Seasons of Life*, Portland, OR: Multnomah Press, 1983.